THE
AFRO-YANKEES

Contributions in Afro-American and African Studies
Series Adviser: Hollis R. Lynch

Freedom and Prejudice: The Legacy of Slavery in
the United States and Brazil
Robert Brent Toplin

The World of Black Singles: Changing Patterns of
Male/Female Relations
Robert Staples

Survival and Progress: The Afro-American Experience
Alex L. Swan

Blood and Flesh: Black American and African Identifications
Josephine Moraa Moikobu

From Du Bois to Van Vechten:The Early New Negro Literature,
1903-1926
Chidi Ikonne

About My Father's Business: The Life of Elder Michaux
Lillian Ashcraft Webb

War and Race: The Black Officer in the American Military,
1915-1941
Gerald W. Patton

The Politics of Literary Expression: A Study of Major
Black Writers
Donald B. Gibson

Science, Myth, Reality: The Black Family
in One-Half Century of Research
Eleanor Engram

Index to *The American Slave*
Donald M. Jacobs, editor

Black Americans and the Missionary Movement in Africa
Sylvia M. Jacobs, editor

Ambivalent Friends: Afro-Americans View the Immigrant
Arnold Shankman

THE AFRO-YANKEES

Providence's Black Community in the Antebellum Era

ROBERT J. COTTROL

CONTRIBUTIONS IN AFRO-AMERICAN AND
AFRICAN STUDIES, NUMBER 68

GREENWOOD PRESS
WESTPORT, CONNECTICUT • LONDON, ENGLAND

Library of Congress Cataloging in Publication Data

Cottrol, Robert J.
  The Afro-Yankees.

  (Contributions in Afro-American and African Studies,
ISSN 0069-9624 ; no. 68)
    Bibliography: p.
    Includes index.
    1. Afro-Americans—Rhode Island—Providence—History.
2. Providence (R.I.)—History. 3. Providence (R.I.)—
Race relations. I. Title. II. Series.
F89.P99N425   974.5'200496073   81-23717
ISBN 0-313-22936-8 (lib. bdg.)   AACR2

Library of Congress Catalog Card Number: 81-23717
ISBN: 0-313-22936-8
ISSN: 0069-9624

First published in 1982

Greenwood Press
A division of Congressional Information Service, Inc.
88 Post Road West
Westport, Connecticut 06881

Printed in the United States of America

10 9 8 7 6 5 4 3 2 1

To My Mother, Father, and Sister

CONTENTS

FIGURES

TABLES

FOREWORD

Most studies of antebellum Afro-American culture and of black-white relations in the United States are concerned, most appropriately, with the southern states. It was in the South that the great majority of the black population lived and worked, and blacks represented over one-third of the region's people. In the northern states slavery had never been a significant economic institution, and the blacks that were enslaved generally worked on small units, often in urban areas, and their occupations were more similar to those of the whites than were those of the slaves on southern plantations. Blacks accounted for only a small part of the region's population, and by the early nineteenth century all of the New England states, as well as the Middle Atlantic states of New York, New Jersey, and Pennsylvania, had provided for the emancipation of their slaves. In some cases emancipation was immediate; more frequently it was to be accomplished by a gradual process with the children born to slave mothers being considered legally free.

Despite this relative numerical unimportance, however, it is clear that studies of the antebellum northern black community are quite important in understanding the evolving pattern of race relations and the emergence of black society and culture in the United States. As *The Afro-Yankees* demonstrates, such studies are useful not only for what they can reveal about northern society .

in the antebellum period, but also in providing a background for examining the range of adjustments that occurred in the aftermath of the emancipation of the southern slaves, both within the South and with the subsequent northward migration. tion.

In tracing the history of Rhode Island's slaves and free blacks from the seventeenth century until the Civil War, Robert J. Cottrol has examined a wide variety of primary sources. He has drawn upon black autobiographies, church and organizational records, convention minutes, personal papers, newspapers, and traveler reports, in addition to the manuscript schedules of federal censuses, state and city census reports, tax lists, probate inventories, city directories, and military muster rolls. These sources are used to detail the changing relations between white attitudes and black behavior and belief, and the developments within the black community. Cottrol relates these factors to the emerging patterns of social and economic change in Rhode Island, and provides a particularly interesting description of the impact of the process of industrialization on race relations in the first half of the nineteenth century.

Rhode Island shippers and merchants had played an important role in the North American slave trade, but, within the state, blacks generally accounted for less than 10 percent of the population. After the Revolutionary War the share of blacks declined with each census, despite some in-migration from other states, falling below 3 percent by 1840. Slavery had been weakened by the passage of a gradual emancipation act in 1784, and by 1800 slaves were less than 1 percent of the state's total population, about one-tenth of the black population. As those still considered slaves aged and died, and with their offspring regarded as free, the number and proportion of slaves declined dramatically in subsequent decades, with only five slaves listed in the 1840 Census, prior to final abolition in 1842. Nevertheless in 1850, of the northern states in which slavery had been ended, only New Jersey had a larger proportion of blacks in the population than did Rhode Island.

Yet, as described by Cottrol, there were significant changes in the conditions of blacks in Rhode Island, and the small black community was at times the focus of major political, social, and

economic battles. In certain ways the legal rights and economic
opportunities of free blacks became more restricted in the nineteenth century, at the time when Rhode Island society was becoming more open for whites (or at least, as the peculiarities of
the voting provisions of 1842 indicated, native-born whites).
Earlier restricted from the militia, Rhode Island's blacks lost
their right to vote in 1822. And, while the ability to vote was
restored in 1842, by the conservative Law and Order party in
the aftermath of the Dorr rebellion, schooling in the urban areas
remained segregated until after the Civil War. Thus the smallness
of numbers, and the inability to pose any major threat to white
domination, did not mean the absence of controls over the free
black population.

The examination of black economic and social life is quite
revealing. That most black workers were in unskilled occupations is not surprising, nor are the slightly more favorable circumstances of mulattoes; yet it is striking that there were so
few blacks employed in the emerging factories and in industrial
occupations. As was to occur in the South at the end of the
nineteenth century, blacks remained within the older occupations, including personal service, and were not able to take
advantage of opportunities in the modernizing sectors that
were to become the basis of continued economic expansion.
Those blacks who were able to acquire even limited amounts
of wealth were generally manual workers, not professionals,
suggesting that it was mainly by frugal living that property accumulation was possible. Despite relatively unfavorable economic conditions, however, most blacks lived in two-parent
households and achieved high levels of literacy.

Cottrol presents a sensitive analysis of the development
of the black community, its separate churches, temperance
and uplift societies, and schools, and the manner in which they
were influenced by white society. In some cases there were aids
provided by whites, but a more typical pattern was conflict
and exclusion. There was apparently little residential segregation and blacks were able to form active protest groups on
various issues, but economically, politically, and socially blacks
were affected by white racism. A separate black community
developed, but this reflected in some measure, "a common

recognition of a common plight," and Cottrol concludes that "the community's identity was not a result of lack of cultural similarity with the white population, but rather the result of white prejudice."

The Afro-Yankees describes a small black community in a small northern state. Yet it provides us with much information about race relations and black life in the antebellum United States. Providence, Rhode Island was in some ways unique, but in many ways its patterns were similar to those seen (and to be seen) elsewhere in the North as well as in the South. Local studies, as Cottrol demonstrates, can tell us a great deal about wider historical patterns.

Stanley L. Engerman
University of Rochester

ACKNOWLEDGMENTS

When I first began reading academic studies I used to marvel at the number of people that authors felt obliged to thank. I now wonder how anything can be written without the acknowledgments section taking up the major portion of one's work, detailing the large number of professional and personal debts acquired during the course of a study. John Blassingame, Kai Erikson, and Sidney Ahlstrom provided the insight, criticism, and support critical to guiding this work through its early stages. I shall always owe a special debt to these three men for devoting time from their busy schedules to consider this work and for their efforts to impart to me their considerable historical and sociological sensitivities. John Blassingame was especially valuable as a critic and mentor. His vast knowledge of Afro-American history and his belief in thorough and rigorous exploration of sources laid a foundation for this study for which I am extremely grateful.

While fashioning this study, my professional debts to other historians continued to accumulate. Portions of this work have been delivered at sessions of the American Historical Association, the Organization of American Historians, the Southern Anthropological Society, and the Washington Area Economic History Seminar. I greatly benefited from the insights and criticisms offered in the ensuing discussions. A number of scholars have taken time from their own pressing research to read manuscripts at various stages of the development of this work and to offer valuable suggestions that have improved this study and reduced its errors. William McFeely, Ira Berlin, and James Horton read and commented extensively on an earlier version of the manuscript, significantly aiding the revision process. Jon Wakelyn acted as my editor for Greenwood Press, encouraging my efforts and contributing his historical insights to my efforts. This work has also been the beneficiary of critical readings and helpful suggestions by Dana White, Delores Aldridge, and Bainbridge Cowell. Finally I must acknowledge a strong professional debt to Stanley Engerman, not only for his generous statements concerning this study but for his sensitive reading of the manuscript and his valuable suggestions, which have greatly enhanced both this work's substance and presentation.

This study would not have been possible without other assistance. Librarians at Beincke and Sterling libraries at Yale University and Woodruff Library at Emory University were especially cooperative, greatly easing the task that I had. I owe a special debt of thanks to Mrs. Rowena Stewart and the staff of the Rhode Island Black Heritage Society and Mrs. Nancy Chudacoff and the staff of the Rhode Island Historical Society for assisting me in finding primary materials. Faculty grants from Emory and Georgetown universities helped defray travel and typing expenses. Personal friends helped with the proofreading and checking the inevitable nagging details: Robert Phelan, Jr., Sharon White, Kevin Thomas, Donald Gastwirth, Stephen P. McGrath, R. Bruce Burke, Jerold Seeman, and Richard Fiesta. More than once their contribution went beyond the correction of some syntactical lapse and into helpful suggestions on substantive issues. Also, I would like to express my appreciation to Arlene Belzer and the production staff at Greenwood Press for their efforts.

As I hope I have made clear, my debts to others in this effort have been considerable. Nonetheless, faults in this study remain my own.

THE
AFRO-YANKEES

INTRODUCTION

Hearing a soft jazz version of Cole Porter's "Night and Day"
is for some the greatest rapture; others demand a shrieking,
ear-piercing, all-consuming, psychedelic, funky soul beat.
Some can envision salvation only within the hierarchical and
authoritarian Roman Catholic church; most attend a simple
Baptist or Methodist service; others seek faiths that will re-
kindle dormant memories of a departed African past. The
choppy franglais patois of their New Brunswick-descended
French Canadian neighbors may be heard from the lips of a
small portion; others have blended an African dialect with
the English of the Stuart and later periods; some have developed
a uniquely black American accent, with rural southern and
northern variants; others speak in regional accents indistinguish-
able from those of their white neighbors. A number parade with
veterans' associations commemorating their previous roles at
Maison en Champagne, Bougainville, Pusan, or Khe Sahn; others
curse the nation that demanded those sacrifices. An upright
clenched fist and a complex handshake seal the bond between
some; a barely perceptible nod of the head indicates the ties
connecting others. Their differences are great, yet black people
in the United States share a culture and are part of a community.
    There is a self-consciousness holding the diverse elements of

the black community together; recognition of and response to racism is the shared pattern of behavior in that community. Well or ill-acculturated to larger American norms, rich or poor, acclaimed or modest, black people in the United States individually and collectively have had as their primary identification a racial label, with other attributes noted as secondary characteristics. Euro-America's collective labeling of the Afro-American population has continually forced Afro-Americans to regard each other as part of a community from the seventeenth and eighteenth centuries, when Africans with varying customs and languages accommodated to the New World and to each other, to the present when black people with contrasting ideologies and life-styles recognize common problems, if not common solutions.

Much attention has been given to the South's role in the forging of this Afro-American culture and community. Most Americans have some mental picture of the antebellum southern plantations where much of Afro-American culture developed. Considerable attention has been given to the effect of the plantation on the development of black social organization. Are present-day Afro-American speech patterns more beholden to Africa or to the plantation? What about the family? Religion? Housing patterns? Political organization? Few have looked at contemporary black life without acknowledging the plantation and trying to assign it either a dominant or major subordinate role (compared to Africa) in the molding of Afro-American national character.

Less attention has been paid to a smaller presence in the Afro-American chronicle; those blacks who lived in the North prior to the Civil War. Their story parallels the southern and national stories; it contained slavery, emancipation, discrimination, resistance, statutory equality, and an unceasing effort to cause statutory equality and social reality to coincide.

If the northern story parallels the southern story, what then has been the northern Afro-American's contribution to black cultu in the United States? It could hardly be argued that the behavioral patterns developed in northern cities and farms are more representative of American Negro culture than those that developed on the plantations and farms of the South, where the overwhelm-

ing majority of antebellum blacks lived. If Afro-American
ethnicity lies not in cultural peculiarities, unique symbols de-
lineating the boundaries between Afro- and Euro-America, but
instead in a common recognition of a common plight, then an
examination of black life in the region where general emancipation was first attained becomes appropriate. It was in the
North that free blacks first had the liberty to operate on their
perception of a common plight. Free Negroes lived in the South,
but white fears that political activity on their part would encourage slave rebelliousness curtailed their institutional independence.[1] Thus it fell on northern blacks to develop the African Methodist Episcopal churches, the black temperance societies, and the Conventions of People of Color that became the
institutional bases for the postemancipation black community.[2]

The formation of the Afro-American community began with
slavery. An empty continent as bereft of labor as it was abundant
of land prompted northern townsman as well as southern planter
to agree with Emanuel Dowling's letter, written in 1645, to
John Winthrop:

. . . for I do not see how we can thrive until we get into a stock of slaves
sufficient to do all our business, for our children's children will hardly
see this great continent filled with people, so that our servants will still
desire freedom to plant for themselves and not stay but for very great
wages. And I suppose you know very well how we shall maintain twenty
Moors cheaper than one English servant.[3]

So the Afro-American community began forming in the rice
and tobacco plantations of the South and the towns and farms
of the North. First in this adoption of a new identity was the
ascription of a new name, Negro; Ibo, Ashanti, Dahomean,
and the others were to be forgotten.

In Rhode Island and the rest of New England, slaveholding
patterns and the cultures of the Puritan slave masters permitted
the development of a semiautonomous slave culture. The records of colonial New England reveal that slaves had a large
amount of freedom of association, often mingling with lower-
class whites and Indians. Unlike their southern counterparts,
slaves in New England did not perform tasks designated solely

for blacks; instead they labored at the range of occupations performed by all laborers in New England society. The Puritan faith was instilled in the children of black and white New England, and because that faith demanded a reading of the Bible, many slaves were taught to read.

Surviving documents indicate a high degree of acculturation among black New Englanders. The combination of being held in households where there were few slaves, the Puritan-Protestant desire to alter the convert's culture as well as his faith, and the association with whites and Indians transformed the African into a Yankee. While definite Africanisms would persist in southern society well into the nineteenth and twentieth centuries, the end of the eighteenth century saw Africa mostly as a fading memory in the minds of a few older blacks in New England.

The end of the eighteenth century also brought an ambiguous freedom to the New England black population. Not explicitly excluded from the franchise, the jury, and the militia, some blacks in the late eighteenth and early nineteenth centuries managed to exercise these practices of citizenship until, in the nineteenth century, there were successful attempts in many states to restrict these acts of citizenship to white men. As Alexis de Tocqueville observed in 1835:

Whoever has inhabited the United States must perceive that in those parts of the Union in which the Negroes are no longer slaves they have in no wise drawn nearer to the whites, on the contrary, the prejudice of race appears to be stronger in the states that have abolished slavery than in those where it still exists. . . . The electoral franchise has been conferred upon the Negroes in almost all the states in which slavery has been abolished but if they come forward to vote their lives are in danger. If oppressed, they may bring an action at law, but they will find none but whites among their judges; and although they may legally serve as jurors, prejudice repels them from that office.[4]

Foreshadowing events in the early twentieth-century South, discrimination grew in the early nineteenth-century North. Black suffrage was restricted, even eliminated; black and white Protestant denominations developed; separate schools were founded; blacks were excluded from theaters, coaches, and railroad cars; skilled trades were closed to them.

The growth of voting restrictions suggests a paradox. Simultaneous with the removal of the eighteenth-century voting rights of free Negroes came a broadening of the franchise for whites, the advent of universal white manhood suffrage. In his study of black voting in pre-Civil War New York, "The Negro Vote in Old New York," Dixon Ryan Fox explained black New Yorkers' Whig sympathies as a reaction to their enemies, the Democrats, who managed to combine a championing of the common man with an antiblack posture.[5] John Langley Stanley's dissertation, "Majority Tyranny in Tocqueville's America: The Failure of Negro Suffrage in New York State in 1846," challenges Fox's assertions of Whig benevolence toward the free Negro population but supports the idea that it was white working-class areas that were more hostile to black suffrage.[6]

It was in pre-Civil War northern communities that patterns of conflict first developed between Afro-Americans and working-class whites. This pattern has persisted to the present and has been an ironic feature in American social history, as two communities with much in common have found themselves as frequently adversaries as allies. An examination of eighteenth-century America indicates that in both North and South, slaves and indentured servants were frequently working at the same tasks, associating freely, recognizing their common bondage more than their differences. This changed in the nineteenth century as white workingmen, particularly Irish immigrants, became the clients of the Democratic party, while the black population placed their loyalties with the more aristocratic Whig party. This pattern of an alliance between blacks seeking betterment and upper-class white sympathizers positioned against working-class whites hostile to black advancement has become a perennial theme in American racial history.

Other responses and adaptations originated in the antebellum North. As Harold Cruse has noted in *The Crisis of the Negro Intellectual*, the twentieth-century integrationist-separatist debate was foreshadowed by the conflicts between such antebellum northern black figures as Frederick Douglass and Martin Delaney.[7] Separatists, ranging from back-to-Africa advocates to those who desired separate institutions that would develop black leaders, as a natural consequence of the all-black character of these institutions, debated integrationists who saw full equality under the American system as the only solution to the nation's racial problem. In looking at those opposing figures then and their modern intellectual and ideological heirs, one still strains to decide who was radical, who accommodationist, who practical, who visionary.

Much of the pattern of antebellum northern discrimination and black response and community development can be seen in the history of Providence, Rhode Island. In his article, "The Providence Negro Community, 1820-1841," Julian Rammelkamp documents the growth of community solidarity among the Providence black community. His study and census figures show that the newly freed people of the late eighteenth and early nineteenth centuries lived as servants among their former masters, accepting a subordinate role in white society. Rammelkamp attributes the formation of black organizations to a rising black consciousness in the early nineteenth century.[8]

Rammelkamp's view of the development of black consciousness did not explore this turning inward as a reaction to the heightened racial regulation that free Negroes encountered in the 1820s. Throughout the nation, the erection of barriers set the free Negro apart from the rest of the population. One manifestation of this tendency occurred in 1822 when Rhode Island restricted the suffrage to free white men. Viewed against this background of increased discrimination, the formation of black community spirit in Providence becomes less the semi-spontaneous phenomenon reported by Rammelkamp and more a defensive reaction to an increasingly hostile white society.

Turning inward to confront the problems faced by it and other free black communities, Providence's black population organized to meet its needs. Abolitionism and the equal-rights struggle, temperance and moral uplift became the concerns of Providence's Afro-Americans.

Access to the franchise was a strong concern of antebellum free Negroes. Rhode Island's movement to eliminate the property qualification for white voters, the Dorr movement, was initially greeted with enthusiasm by blacks and their leader, Thomas Wilson Dorr. This initial approval reversed when, despite the egalitarian impulses of Dorr, the rank and file of the Suffrage party expressed opposition to black suffrage.

At this point Rhode Island became the scene of one of the many confrontations between blacks and lower-class whites in the nation's history. Spurned by lower-class whites, native and foreign born, who were seeking the franchise for themselves but whose prejudice did not let them see the desirability of extending the privilege beyond the white race, blacks aligned themselves with the freeholders. Black militiamen mustered to control the rebellious suffrage advocates. In return for this support, the freeholders reinstated the black vote in 1842.

A black culture developed in pre-Civil War Providence. Similar to black cultures in other northern cities, it was not dissimilar to the surrounding white culture. Christian, democratic, and thrifty, it had seamen, teachers, preachers, entrepreneurs, military company paraders; black residents of Providence developed institutions that paralleled white ones. The community's identity was not a result of lack of cultural similarity with the white population but rather the result of white prejudice. This is the story of that community.

Notes

1. Ira Berlin, *Slaves Without Masters* (New York: Vintage Books, 1974), p. 286.

2. E. Franklin Frazier, *The Negro Church in America* (New York: Schocken Books, 1974).

3. Elizabeth Donnan, *Documents Illustrative of the History of the Slave Trade to America*, vol. 3 (Washington, D.C.: Carnegie Institute, 1932), p. 8.

4. Alexis de Tocqueville, *Democracy in America*, vol. 1 (New York: Vintage Books, 1945), pp. 373-74.

5. Dixon Ryan Fox, "The Negro Vote in Old New York," in *Free Blacks in America 1800-1860*, ed. John H. Bracey, Elliott Rudwick, and August Meier (Belmont, Calif.: Wadsworth Publishers, 1970), pp. 95-112.

6. John Langley Stanley, "Majority Tyranny in Tocqueville's America: The Failure of Negro Suffrage in New York State in 1846" (Ph.D. diss., Cornell University, 1966).

7. Harold Cruse, *The Crisis of the Negro Intellectual* (New York: William Morrow & Co., 1967).

8. Julian Rammelkamp, "The Providence Negro Community 1820-1841," in *Free Blacks in America*, pp. 85-94.

SLAVERY AND COMMUNITY IN PROVIDENCE AND NEW ENGLAND

1

Something happened in America. Somewhere between the landing of "twenty Negars" at Jamestown in 1619 and the early years of the nineteenth century, the old English social divisions of class, religion, and ethnicity were subordinated to a new American distinction—race. Not the least important result of this metamorphosis was the formation of a self-aware Afro-American community. For all Americans, race was to become an ever-present consideration affecting and defining the boundaries of social interaction. Black Americans were to be most conditioned by this American social distinction; it was this conditioning that forged the links between disparate Africans and their diverse Afro-American descendants, creating a community.

This did not happen at once. Indeed even as late as the Revolutionary War era, such community as existed among blacks was embryonic, lacking both the catholicity and political impetus that would be the hallmark of the decades and centuries that were to follow. The modern black community did not appear overnight. Time, contact, and demography changed the African into an Afro-American. Yet more than the passage of time was responsible for the development of black consciousness, and it was not simply the shortness of the Afro-American odyssey in the colonial era that augured for the limited community of that period. The less sharp racial differentiation of the colonial centuries (compared to the nineteenth and twentieth centuries) and the absence of a reasonably independent black social life combined to mute, on any major scale, the communal impulses of a people in a common predicament.

Racial distinctions in colonial America were less pronounced than they would become. This was not because early America had a high regard for black bondsmen but rather because many whites were also in bondage. Recruited from the British lower classes, frequently the Irish, whites held in various forms of servitude often lived lives that were little different from those of black slaves. Indentured servants, apprentices, and seamen worked at the same occupations that slaves did, were sold on auction blocks alongside imported Africans, and were flogged and maimed for many of the same offenses for which blacks were punished. Newspapers in colonial America often carried advertisements for both runaway blacks and runaway whites. Only the duration of their servitude separated black from white bondsmen.

Class prejudice and xenophobia helped secure the white servant's lowly place in colonial America. Historians have noted the sense of uniqueness felt by sixteenth- and seventeenth-century Englishmen. Middle-class Englishmen of the Stuart period had a chauvinistic democratic sense that allowed them to demand political and ecclesiastical liberty for themselves, while they denied such freedoms to others. Whether Winthrop Jordan's view that English culture was predisposed toward anti-black prejudice is accurate is less important for the study of early colonial race relations than the fact that the English were hostile to many European groups. Protestant, convinced of the peculiarity of their liberties, it took little to persuade seventeenth-century Englishmen of the inferiority of their European neighbors, who were largely Catholic and governed by less enlightened political arrangements. They hated the Irish. The English were also quite willing to extend their contempt to those in English society who were destitute or forced into crime because of their poverty. With so many objects of scorn so close at hand, it seems unlikely that the African, at least initially, was considered much worse in the English mind than many Europeans were. Thus, the destitute English orphan, the convict offered the choice between exile in the New World or the gallows, and the Irish victim of Cromwell's subjugation of his island would all become the servants in the Americas, the people who would occupy the same physical and nearly the same social space as the African slaves.[1]

In every English colony white servants could be seen working alongside black slaves. From the sugar cane fields of Jamaica to the tobacco plantations of Virginia and the shops and farms of New England, black and white picked crops, worked metal, and constructed houses and ships together. Sometimes there was a division of labor between black and white. Where there was a large slave population and a consequent fear of slave rebellion, white servants were frequently elevated. They supervised black slaves and helped to maintain the dominance of the masters over blacks in bondage. In places where masters were secure in their control, however, there was little elevation of whites in bondage. Instead during their period of servitude, their lives were very much like those of slaves.

In New England the drama of servant and slave, black and white, played. Few of the survivors of the middle passage came there. Unable, despite the brisk Yankee slaving business, to snare more victims of the African trade than its Caribbean neighbors, British North America imported relatively few slaves, small-enterprise New England fewer still. The relatively small number of Africans, and later Afro-Americans, present in New England society was to affect the region's development as a multiracial society, as well as its contribution to national racial questions.

From the beginning, Rhode Islanders and the other New Englanders were uncomfortable with slavetrading and slave-holding. Man-stealing was wrong; the Old Testament-reading Puritans knew this ancient prohibition. Yet the New England mind did allow an exception: the captive taken in a just war. He was to be beyond the protection of the Mosaic code.[2]

Amerindians, not Africans, became the first victims of the "just war exception." Captives in the Pequot War of 1637 provided New England's first slaves. The war also introduced New England to the slave trade. Female captives and children were sold as slaves in New England, while male captives were traded in the West Indies for partially acculturated Africans.[3]

Slaving became a substantial New England enterprise. Prosecutions against man-stealing occurred in Massachusetts despite the acknowledged legitimacy of buying the losers of just wars. Newport, Bristol, and Providence were to become major slave-trading centers even though the Rhode Island general court on May 19, 1652, stated:

Whereas, there is a common course practiced amongst Englishmen to buy Negars, to that end that they may have them for service or slaves forever; for the preventing of such practices among us, let it be ordered that no black mankind or white be forced by covenant bond, or otherwise, to serve any man or his assignes longer than ten years.

Yet black mankind did serve longer than ten years in Rhode Island and elsewhere in New England. New England shipowners supplied West Indian planters with African slaves, bringing home the surplus captives to work in New England. Children and other not likely to fetch a high price in the labor-intensive West Indies and slaves seasoned in the West Indies, acculturated to European ways, and, hence, more valuable to New Englanders, came to Rhode Island and neighboring Massachusetts and Connecticut.[4]

The first blacks brought to Rhode Island were not slaves. The anti-slavery sentiments expressed by the Rhode Island court in 1652 were adhered to for a time. Instead, for most of the seventeenth century, they were treated as servants and released after ten years. Rhode Island's opposition to slavery was also indicated by a law passed in 1675 that prohibited the enslavement of Indians.[5]

By the early years of the eighteenth century, however, Rhode Island had become a major slavetrading center. Newport was the second largest slavetrading port in New England, rivaled only by Boston. The wealth of Newport rested on its maritime trade. Its rum distilleries provided the medium of exchange that would be used to procure West Africans for West Indian plantations. At first, Newport traders sold their human cargoes almost exclusively in the West Indies. Blacks who were imported into Rhode Island tended to come from Barbados instead. In 1708, Samuel Cranston, then governor of Rhode Island, noted that between 1698 and 1707 no Africans had been imported into Rhode Island

But the growth of the African trade inevitably meant that this would change. Merchants in the slave trade wanted house servants. Captains of slaving vessels were permitted by vessel owners to reserve some of their cargo for themselves. These captains found a ready market for slaves in the expanding commercial towns of Newport and Providence. They also found a heavy demand on the large farms of southern Rhode Island.[6]

In 1708, Rhode Island recognized the significance of African importation by levying a three pound tax on each slave brought into the colony. The sum could be returned if a newly imported slave was immediately exported out of Rhode Island. One of the original motivations for the tax seems to have been an effort to limit the size of the nonwhite population. In 1715, there was an outright prohibition on the importation of Indian slaves. The following reason was given:

... divers conspiracies, insurrections, rapes, thefts and other exerable crimes have been lately perpetrated in this and the adjoining governments by Indian slaves, *and the increase of them in this colony daily discourages the importation of white servants from Great Britain.*

The preference for white servants partially motivated Rhode Island's tax on imported slaves.[7]

But the tax did not stop the importation. So many slaves were imported that enough taxes were collected to pay for public works in Newport. In 1717, an ordinance was passed that took one hundred pounds out of the import fund to pay for paving Newport's streets. In 1729, it was ordered that half of the monies taken from this import tax would be used to repair the streets of Newport. The British crown, feeling that the import tax might harm the slave trade, repealed the tax in 1732.[8]

Despite the import tax, the Rhode Island black population grew. The following list indicates the growth of the white and black populations of Rhode Island as the colony developed in the eighteenth century.[9]

Providence was not the major market for slaves in Rhode Island in the eighteenth century. As in many other areas of eighteenth-century Rhode Island life, Providence's develop-

Table 1-1
WHITE AND BLACK POPULATION GROWTH IN RHODE ISLAND

YEAR	WHITE	BLACK	PERCENTAGE BLACK
1708	7,181	425	5.6
1730	17,935	1,648	8.4
1749	32,773	3,077	8.6
1756	35,939	4,697	11.6
1774	59,707	3,668	5.8

SOURCE: William D. Johnson, *Slavery in Rhode Island, 1755-1776*, Rhod
Island Historical Society Publications, vol. 2 (Providence: Rhode Island
Historical Society, 1894), p. 127.

ment in both slavetrading and slaveholding was overshadowed
by Newport. The wealthier merchants of Newport held more
slaves than the upper classes of Providence. The planters in the
southern part of Rhode Island also held more slaves than the
masters of Providence. Of the 3,668 blacks listed in the 1774
census, 1,246 lived in Newport. South Kingstown had the
second largest black population with 404 blacks listed, while
Providence had only the third largest black population—303.[10]

There were three patterns of slaveholding in colonial Rhode
Island. In wealthy, commercial Newport, most slaves were employed as house servants. In the southern part of the state, slav
worked the Narragansett plantations, with some Narragansett
planters owning as many as forty slaves who worked alongside
whites and Narragansett Indian servants producing wool, dairy
products, corn, and tobacco. They also bred Narragansett pace
racehorses.[11]

In Providence, slaves engaged in a variety of tasks. Some wer
house servants; others worked for shoemakers, blacksmiths, ca
penters, or fishermen. Although occasionally the records show
a former slave who attained some wealth or local tradition preserves the memory of some slave, little information remains of
the lives of most Providence slaves. What does remain can be
enhanced if Providence is viewed not as a unique and isolated
case. Understanding slavery in Providence, and indeed in New
England generally, is in part understanding urban slavery as
something distinct from plantation slavery. The slave's relation

with freemen, his working conditions, and his possibilities for
manumission were different and better in the urban setting
than they were on the plantation. Urban masters owned slaves
in small number; slaves in cities had more contact with persons
outside the master's household. While the plantation might attempt to be a self-contained community, forcing slaves to pick
their associates from other plantation slaves, the urban households with their small number of slaves could not. Unless the
slave in the city was to be friendless and celibate, he had to
be permitted to associate with people who were not under his
master's control. Moreover, the closeness of households in the
city made association outside of the master's domain considera-
bly easier than was the case on plantations, where distance might
limit one's interactions.[12]

A wider circle of acquaintances was one way that the urban
slave's life was different from the plantation slave's; the lack of
a status-defined occupation (that is, a task done only or pre-
dominantly by slaves) was another. The occupations of urban
slaves were similar to those of free laborers, apprentices, and
servants. The skills of slave artisans, seamen, and house servants
were used not only for the benefit of masters but to the slave's
advantage as well. Urban slaves, unlike their rural counterparts,
were able to hire themselves out to work for employers other
than their masters and to earn money. Slaves in cities had the
skills of free society; plantation slaves, the skills of the bonds-
man. As was the case with his social interactions, physical closeness aided the urban slave in his quest for outside employment.

Slaves in cities had a wider range of life options as slaves
than did their plantation counterparts. The absence of rigidly
defined slave occupations, the opportunity to earn money, and
the relative freedom of association that the slave had in the city
all contributed to the urban slave's living a life that, in many
ways, was not markedly different from that of the free lower
classes. Because of their ability to earn money, slaves were sometimes able to purchase their freedom. In British and Latin America, the city became the dwelling place of the free Negro because
it was the place where the evolution from semiautonomous slave
artisan to free man could take place.

New England's masters owned slaves on a small scale. The

slave populations of Massachusetts, Connecticut, and Rhode Island were small. Lorenzo Johnston Greene in *The Negro in Colonial New England* places the black population at the following: Massachusetts (1776), 5,249, or 1.8 percent of the population; Rhode Island (1775), 3,761, or 6.3 percent of the population; and Connecticut 6,464, or 3.2 percent of the population. The Rhode Island census of 1774 indicates that no master in Providence had more than 7 slaves in his household. Of the 4,321 persons in Providence that year, 303 were black and 68 were Indians. Of the 655 families in Providence, 20 families were headed by free blacks or Indians. One hundred and sixty-six of the 635 white-headed households had Indian or black servants or slaves, roughly 26 percent of the families. Of slaveholding households, 57, or 34 percent, were listed as having just one slave. Seventy-three percent, or 122 slaveholding families, had 5 slaves or less.[13] (See figure 1-1.)

Although the economies of the New England colonies never presented the financial opportunities that gave rise to the plantation empires of the southern or West Indian colonies, there were advantages to employing slaves. In New England it was difficult to recruit people to that class of laborers that included farm hands, artisans' assistants, house servants, and seamen. Youthful apprentices and indentured servants might be made to assume these roles for a time, but masters could hope to employ such people only as long as age or indenture contract prevailed. As Downing lamented, plentiful land meant scarce servants. In Providence and the rest of New England, property owners at an early stage appreciated the value of the slave.[14]

Engaged in tasks similar to those of the white lower classes, slaves associated with their co-workers. They worshipped, drank, fought, rioted, and loved with a closeness that belied their differing statuses, despite public ordinances that sought to curtail such examples of black independence. The absence of social control agents charged with a specific responsibility for slave discipline allowed ambivalent enforcement of those ordinances. Continuous repetition of such edicts indicates their minimal success.[15]

The unsanctioned, illicit gathering places of the lower classes were places of black-white equality. Throughout eighteenth-century New England, the disorders caused by "boys and Ne-

Figure 1-1

Slaveholding in Providence, 1774

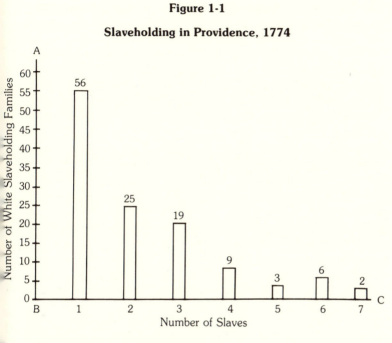

Source: Rhode Island Census, 1774, pp. 38-53.

groes" was a constant lament. Colonial records abound with
legislative attempts to stop this fraternization and to halt the
disorders that slave and servant fomented. As early as 1649,
the town of Providence sought to force masters to control
their slaves by making masters responsible for any damage
done by servants. The Rhode Island legislature in 1703 passed
laws prohibiting blacks and Indians from being out after
9:00 P.M. In 1708, the colony passed an ordinance prohibiting home owners from entertaining Negroes without their masters'
permission. Evidently in Providence, one of the unsanctioned
gathering places of slave and bonded white was the town water
pump where slave boys and indentured servants drew water.
There, friendships and animosities developed as personalities
dictated, and the mischiefs of both groups alarmed the city's
rulers.[16]

Blacks and whites also gathered at taverns. The August 12,
1761, lamentation to the Boston selectmen indicates both the

dismay with which this practice was viewed and the repeated nature of such offenses:

> Ordered that several retailers within this town be *once more informed and notified* that in any case they should hence forward sell or deliver rum and other spiritous liquors to Negro and Mullatto servants, not bringing certificates from their masters or shall allow persons to sit tippling in their houses; they may depend upon being dealt with according to the severity of the law.[17]

The *Providence Gazette* of September 1, 1770, reveals that Providence officials were also concerned with black tippling. An article reported the lament of the town council that free Negroes and mulattoes were keeping disorderly houses, enticing slaves to spend time and money in disreputable activities. The resolution went on to prescribe that

> any free Negro or mulatto who shall keep a disorderly house, or entertain any slave or slaves at unreasonable hours or in any flagrant manner, such town council be hereby empowered to examine into said matter . . . and shall find such free Negro or mulatto guilty of the same. They may, if they think proper, break up from house-keeping such free Negro or mulatto. And if such free Negroes or mulattoes have been slaves and manumitted by their masters . . . town councils are hereby empowered . . . to put out and bind them as servants for a term of time, not exceeding four years.[18]

Connecticut lawmakers had similar misgivings about slaves' frequenting public houses and consequently passed an ordinance i 1703 forbidding Negroes and servants from drinking in public houses without their masters' permission.

Boston mobs provide a picture of the integration of slaves an free Negroes with lower-class whites. Crispus Attucks's role in the Boston Massacre is well known. Equally relevant is black in clusion in the Pope's Day celebrations. The *Boston Gazette*'s descriptions of the 1765 Pope's Day celebrations show a riotou crowd composed of "servants and Negroes." Rival mobs from the north end and south end, apparently integrated, fought eac other for reasons now long obscured. Slaves were initially at liberty to join these celebrations, but the *Gazette* goes on to record that later on a curfew was placed on the slaves in an attempt to stem riotous behavior.[19]

Slaves met with whites in places that did not have New England society's approval; they also met in one area that did; the church. As was the case throughout British America, masters initially were reluctant to convert their slaves, fearing that Christianity might mandate freedom; but in New England that conflict was resolved early. Slaves were converted, became full members of churches, and remained in bondage.

Religious revivals and periods of intense religiosity saw black and white converts come to the meetings of ministers to receive salvation. The Reverend Jonathan Edwards noted the black and Indian presence at his revivals: "There are several Negroes, that from what was seen in them then, and what is discernible in them since, appear to have been truly born again in the late remarkable season."[20] He also noted:

And under the influence of this work, there have been many of the remains of those wretched people and dregs of mankind, the poor Indians . . . forsaken forever their forever stupid, barbarous and brutish ways of living . . . and many of the poor Negroes have been in like manner wrought upon and changed.[21]

Association outside of the master's household made miscegenation possible. Despite the law's discouragement, black and white made love in and out of wedlock. Interracial sex was hardly an anomaly wherever slavery occurred, but New England stands out because of the large number of relationships between black men and white women. In a letter written in 1795 in Massachusetts, the Reverend John Eliot indicated that much of the furor over blacks in public houses may have been an attempt to preclude sexual contact between black men and white women:

There is much harmony between blacks and whites. We seldom have contentions except in houses of ill-fame where some very depraved white females get among the blacks. This has issued in the pulling down of such houses at times and has caused several actions at Justices Courts these two years past.[22]

Evidence of interracial marriage between male slaves and free or servant white females exists. Eighteenth-century Boston marriage records put the term *Negro* before or after the names of blacks, but clerks recording marriages did not use a consistent system in identifying Negroes, thus creating a problem in determining which marriages were interracial. Four ways of noting black intraracial marriages were used: John Negro and Betty Negro; John and Betty, both Negroes; Negroes John and Betty; and Negro John and Negro Betty. In several cases in the records, *Negro* is used to describe only one partner: Derham Negro and Grace (1701), Negro Phillip and Betty (1703), John Negro and Betty Tippet (1705), James Richard Negro and Betty Pow (1705), Jack Negro and Sue (1705), Robin Negro and Kate (1705), and Robin Negro and Moll (1705).[23] During these years other marriages were recorded duly noting that both partners were black. Lorenzo Johnston Greene, viewing similarly ambiguous evidence in *Early Connecticut Marriages and Early Massachusetts Marriages*, came to the conclusion that some of the marriages in which one partner was noted as black while the other was not probably were interracial.[24]

There is evidence of some black-white marriages in Charlestowne, Rhode Island, but it is difficult to assess whether such marriages occurred in Providence. The 1774 census shows blacks living in white households but does not break down the black population by age or sex, thus ending further speculation. The federal census of 1790 shows whites living in the same household with free blacks, but without the kind of detail that would suggest either a master-servant or more intimate kind of relationship.[25]

Black-Indian marriages were frequent in Rhode Island. Such unions were not discouraged by law even though most of the native Narragansetts were free. William Brown, a nineteenth-century black businessman and political leader, whose grandmother Alice Prophet was a Narragansett, observed that some Indian women may have preferred marrying black men as a means of escaping the rigors that life presented to the Narragansett woman:[26]

It was customary for the woman to do all the drudgery and hard work indoors and out. The Indian men thought it a disgrace to work; they thought they did their part by hunting and procuring game. The Indian women observing the colored men working for their wives, and living after the man-

ner of white people in comfortable homes, felt anxious to change their position in life; not being able to carry out their designs in any other way, re-
sorted to making purchases. This created a very bitter feeling among the
Indian men against the blacks. The treatment the Indian women received
from the husbands they had purchased was so satisfactory that others were
encouraged to follow their example.[27]

Any discussion of slavery in Rhode Island or the rest of New
England would be incomplete without an examination of that
critical social and cultural institution, the African governors'
elections. Probably starting in the late 1730s or early 1740s,
these elections, held among the black population, lasted until
the 1830s in some parts of New England, thus spanning both the
eras of slavery and freedom in the region. Culturally these elections seem to have had a mixed African and Iberian origin. In
New England masters contributed English electoral practices to
these activities. These were mock elections in which slaves com-
peted for local and sometimes statewide offices. Masters were
heavily involved in these elections, bribing slaves with money
and refreshments in order to induce their vote for the master's
candidate, usually a favorite slave. It was a mark of status for
both master and slave if a slave was elected to office. The elections were occasions for holidays and celebrations attended by
slave candidates, their white sponsors, other slaves and sometimes white servants.[28]

These elections simultaneously furnish evidence of an embryonic community impulse among Rhode Island slaves and
of the difficulties of independent community life under slavery.
Status and prestige among slaves in some measure did depend
on success in these ceremonies. Eleanor Eldridge, a black woman who lived in nineteenth-century Providence, recalled that
she and her brother were accorded a high degree of respect
after his election as an African Governor. She also was com-
plimented with a number of suitors after that event. William
Brown noted that election days were well attended by almost
all blacks, except for an ultrareligious minority who objected
to the revelries attendant to such events. Clearly these elections
became activities around which a community focused.[29]

But these elections also indicate the master's dominance over
the slave's activities. Orville H. Platt in his essay "Negro Gover-

nors" noted that masters in Connecticut used these slave official to control slaves. Local "justices of the peace," appointed by the slave governors, were used to discipline miscreants. William Brown indicated that masters arranged these elections as labor incentives. Masters would rent out taverns for slaves on election days, usually the third Saturday in June in Rhode Island, supply ing refreshments, knowing that this would spur their slaves to greater efforts at harvesttime. Whether as incentive or means of social control, masters made use of these elections, and their considerable involvement indicates a large degree of white control of one of eighteenth-century Rhode Island's major black social ceremonies.[30]

Contact among slaves and between slave and free, tavern frequenting, and mock elections might have mitigated slavery but did not negate it. Slavery meant being a perpetual servant, staying permanently in a status that was only temporary for white people. Slavery also meant the possibility of family separation, despite society's disapproval. A Massachusetts slave expressed his concerns in a petition for freedom to Governor Thomas Gage

How can a slave perform the duties of a husband to a wife or parent to his child? How can a husband leave master and work and cleave to his wife? How can the wife submit themselves to their husbands in all things? There is a great number of us . . . sincere . . . members of the Church of Christ, how can the master and the slave be said to fulfill that command live in love let brotherly love counter and abound, bear my burden when he bears down with half chains of slavery and oppression against my Will. . . . And we can't serve our God whilst in this situation.[31]

In colonial New England freedom could be attained by either manumission or escape. Seventeenth- and early eighteenth-centu Rhode Island masters frequently set blacks free after a period of servitude. This changed when a 1728 ordinance prohibited the manumission of Rhode Island slaves unless masters first posted a one hundred pound bond to make sure that the freedmen would not become public charges.[32]

Manumissions continued after the 1728 ordinance. Some masters altruistically freed their slaves; others permitted slaves to purchase their freedom. Providence was experiencing commercial growth in the middle of the eighteenth century, and some slaves managed to take advantage of this prosperity to earn money and purchase their freedom. Evidently some slaves in Providence fished and sold their catches to raise money. The Providence records indicate that some slaves turned to business activities in order to acquire money. For example, in 1748, two slaves, one identified as Pompey Brown, the other only as Sam, purchased shares in a privateering vessel. A woman named Ann Lippit purchased Sam's share for him. Many slaves in Providence earned money by working at various jobs and used their earnings to buy their freedom.[33]

We do not have firsthand accounts of blacks in Providence who worked in their spare time and managed to purchase their freedom. There exists, however, the valuable autobiography of a slave who lived in New London County, Connecticut, *A Narrative of the Life and Adventures of Venture, A Native of Africa* by Venture Smith. Smith succeeded in purchasing himself, his wife, his three children, and three other slaves, whom he set free, by hiring himself out. His activities give a clue to the activities in which Providence slaves who managed to free themselves were probably engaged.

Smith, born in Africa and brought to Rhode Island before the age of ten, was put to the task of carding wool by his first American master.[34] He spent his childhood, youth, and young adulthood as a slave in Rhode Island. As a young man, Smith attempted to escape bondage in the company of some other slaves and an Irish indentured servant. The attempt failed, and shortly thereafter Smith was sold to Thomas Stanton of Stonington, Connecticut. Thomas Stanton's brother Robert purchased Smith's wife and children and brought them from Rhode Island to Stonington.

Venture Smith hired himself out to Robert Stanton for the sum of twenty-one pounds per year; Smith's original purchase price, fifty-six pounds, could thus be earned in a short enough number of years to make hiring out a feasible means of attaining freedom. Because of a dispute with the Stantons, Smith lost the money he earned in his year's employment with Robert Stanton. Shortly after this period, Venture was sold to Colonel Smith.[35]

Under Colonel Smith, Venture managed to free himself by

the hiring-out process. Cautious because of the refusal of the Stantons to honor their agreement, Venture Smith left his earnings with a free Negro instead of turning in his money and purchasing himself directly from Colonel Smith. Smith's freedom to associate with a free man played an important part in his attaining freedom.[36]

In addition to working as a laborer, Venture earned money by selling fish. While acquiring money for self-manumission, Smith ran into another pitfall. Colonel Smith, though more trustworthy than the Stantons, nonetheless balked at allowing Venture Smith to hire himself out for one summer session. During that summer Venture had to pay Colonel Smith two pounds a month over and above his manumission price for the privilege of working. In all, Venture Smith paid seventy-one pounds to Colonel Smith for his manumission.[37]

After securing his own freedom, Smith purchased his wife and two sons. Evidently he then went about the task of purchasing and freeing others; after that, they worked off their purchase prices as laborers for him. He wrote, "I had already redeemed from slavery my self, my wife and children, besides three Negro men."[38]

Some chose a different path to freedom. They ran away. One of the more common means of escape for slaves in Providence was to join ships' crews. Several advertisements in the *Providence Gazette* in the 1760s and 1770s warned masters of vessels not to harbor fugitive slaves. In the *Providence Gazette* of November 6, 1779, James Brown advertised for his mulatto slave who had run away, suggesting that the escaped slave might seek work as a privateer. Often advertisements for runaway slaves were placed next to those for runaway seamen, indicating that ships' captains may have needed the services the fugitives offered. Rhode Island masters were so afraid of slaves' escaping to sea that they had an ordinance passed in 1757 giving masters unlimited rights to search vessels for fugitives. This ordinance also prescribed a five hundred pound fine for ships' captains who harbored fugitives on their vessels.[39]

The advertisements for runaway slaves in Providence indicate the degree of acculturation of the Rhode Island slave. These advertisements show a black population that was quite able to function in the New England economy. One such advertisement, in an April 1763 edition of the *Gazette*, was for a slave named York. His master, James Carder, noted that York had forged his master's name on a pass. Carder believed that York was headed for either New York City or Albany. Later that same month another master, Lodwick Updike, offered a reward of six dollars for the return of his slave Dinas. Dinas had also forged a pass, and Updike believed he was headed for Boston. Advertisements for Dinas continued for another month. On July 9, 1763, Daniel Fenner advertised for an escaped thirty-eight-year-old mulatto woman. She was a skilled seamstress, and Fenner feared that she had gone to Boston where many of her friends lived.[40] One advertisement for a runaway that illustrates many of the difficulties Providence masters had in keeping reluctant slaves can be found in the July 22, 1769, edition of the *Providence Gazette:*

Run away from on board a brig lying in the river, a mulatto man, named Francisco, of a middle stature, thick set, speaks broken English: had on a blue jacket, sailors trousers, and took a small hat belonging to one of the people. Whoever takes up said mulatto and brings him to the subscriber, shall have two dollars reward, and necessary charges paid by

John Nash

N.B. he has a sore on his right hand. All masters of vessels are forbid to carry him off.[41]

Francisco's case shows how blurred the lines between lower-class free workers and slaves could be. Francisco was definitely familiar with the nautical life. He ran away from a brig. His dress was that of a sailor. His name and broken English suggest that he previously came from the Caribbean or some other part of Latin America. Was he a slave employed on a boat or a dissatisfied sailor? His master does not specifically mention that Francisco was a slave. Yet would John Nash have been worried that a free sailor would escape on another vessel? Whatever the answers to these questions, Francisco was a mulatto runaway who could clearly function as a free man in New England.

Another case, not of a runaway but of a missing slave, again illustrates this point of blurred distinctions and the possibilities of slave escape:

Missing—Quam, a Negro man supposed to be about thirty years of age, by trade a cooper, went from his master's house in Providence (most probably in a delirious condition, being often subject to be so on Sunday), the 8th day of July last, and has not been heard of since.
He is of a middling stature, him makes of a serious thoughtful turn of mind incline to talk but little, but speaks pretty good English, is a good workman, at his trade and formerly lived with Mr. Alexander Frazier, of whom he learned it. Had on an old striped flannel jacket, striped shirt, tan trousers and an old hat, but took nothing else with him that is known although he was uncommonly neat and precise in his dress. Whoever can give any account (if living) where he is, so that his master may have him again, or will (if he is found living) tenderly and kindly treat him and return him as soon as possible to his master shall have two dollars reward and all necessary expenses and charged paid by— Job Smith.[42]

Quam was a highly acculturated black artisan. He appears to have been on very good terms with his master, and that probably speeded the development of his facility in English as well as his skill as a cooper. This advertisement further illustrates the relative freedom of movement enjoyed by the slave in Providence. Quam slipped away without his master noticing it; indeed, if Smith is accurate, without Quam's full knowledge as well. The frequency of runaway advertisements indicates that many blacks were attaining freedom by leaving their masters, usually more purposefully than Quam.

There was a considerable free black population in eighteenth-century Providence. By the census of 1774, of the 303 blacks in Providence, 46 lived in black-headed households and presumably were free. Some people from the beginning treated imported Africans as indentured servants and set them free after specific periods of time. One such case involved William Hawkins who in 1695 informed the Providence town council that he intended to release the black man, Jack, whom he had just purchased, after twenty-six years. Some masters manumitted slaves for humanitarian or personal reasons. Others liberated slaves who were too old to be of any economic value. This situation alarmed the Rhode Island legislature, which considered the prospect of having to support elderly or infirm slaves; the legislature in 1728 dictated that masters had to put up a bond before manumitting slaves.[43]

However they attained freedom, free Negroes were not equal citizens in colonial New England. Rights and privileges accorded whites were denied blacks. Generally black men were denied the vote and public office. Black men were excluded from militia duty, forced instead to serve on public works projects. The only exception was in time of war when emergency and the threat of combat democratized the privilege of bearing arms. Rhode Island muster rolls during the French and Indian wars, for instance, reveal a number of black men serving with Rhode Island forces.[44]

Legal handicaps aside, free Negroes nevertheless were able to engage in a wide range of economic and social activities. The evidence indicates racial integration, free Negroes living among white neighbors. Eighteenth-century Boston selectmen's records show white neighbors suing black neighbors. The Rhode Island census shows free blacks living near whites. Free Negroes could engage in business and had access to the courts to protect their livelihoods. In Providence, one of the more successful free black entrepreneurs was an oyster house owner named Emmanuel, formerly a slave of one Gabriel Bernon. He was manumitted in 1736. Turning to his own use the skills that had previously served his master, Emmanuel plied his food and drink trade with a great deal of success, so much so that when he died in 1769 he left a house and a lot and a personal estate valued at 539 pounds, 10 shillings to his wife.[45]

Initial doubts about the propriety of slavery persisted and grew, but these had to coexist with the profits Rhode Island merchants realized from the African-West Indian slave trade. Moses Brown, whose family was heavily involved in the slave trade, was one of those who came to realize the evils of slaving and slaveholding. As a master, Brown had insisted on marriage as well as religious and secular instruction for his slaves. By 1773, he decided that these were not enough and he announced to the world:

Whereas I am clearly convinced that the buying and selling of men of what color soever as slaves is contrary to the Divine mind manifest in the con-

sciences of all men however some may smother and neglect its reprovings
and being also made sensible that the holding of Negroes in slavery however kindly treated by their masters has a great tendency to encourage the
iniquitous practice of importing them from their native country and is
contrary to that justice, mercy and humanity enjoined as the duty of
every Christian, I do hereby these presents for myself, my heirs etc. manu-
mit and set free the following Negroes.[46]

Brown's convictions were not universally shared. Others clung
to their human property and, perhaps more significantly, their
profits from the slave trade. But the American Revolution was to
alter the perceptions of many on questions of liberty and slavery.
In Rhode Island, as in many other northern colonies, the contra-
diction between revolutionary rhetoric and slaveholding practice
would become too great a strain for both to continue.

Military necessity also contributed to the decline of slavery in
Rhode Island. Rhode Island's inability to enlist sufficient white
troops caused the Rhode Island assembly to permit black enlistment in 1778. In February of that year, the General Assembly
passed an act permitting "the enlistment of "every able-bodied
Negro, Mulatto or Indian man slave" in two battalions the state
was attempting to raise. The act specified that slaves enlisting
in the Rhode Island forces would be discharged from the service
of their owners. Slaves enlisting would be entitled to the same
pay and bounties as white troops, including state support in the
event of illness or injury. Slave owners were to be compensated
at a rate not to exceed 120 pounds for each slave who enlisted.[4]

The measure permitting slave enlistments was protested by a
group of slavetraders and slave owners who contended that the
world would ridicule Rhode Island for the enlistments because
"the state had purchased a band of slaves to be employed in the
defense of the rights and liberties of our country." The protest-
ers also stated that it would cost more to enlist blacks and that
owners would be reluctant to accept the prices offered for slaves.
Despite these objections, Rhode Island decided to raise the two
battalions, under the command of Colonel Christopher Greene.[4]
Despite the intention to raise two battalions, only the equivalent
of one battalion of freedmen appears to have been raised. Estimates of the size of the battalion vary between 130 and 250
men. Records exist that give the names and home towns of 74

of the enlistees. Only 3 of the enlisted freedmen came from
Providence. Forty-five of the 74 came from the Narragansett
area and 6 from Newport. The freedmen enlisted throughout
1778 despite a largely ignored law that sought to curtail black
enlistments that was passed in June of that year. The unit stayed
in active service until 1783.[49]

The battalion the freedmen enlisted in, which has usually been
called "the black regiment or regiment of slaves," won much
praise for its conduct during the battle of Rhode Island. The
promise made in 1778 that those enlisting would receive the
same benefits as whites appears to have been honored. Unfortunately pay and bounties were in the nearly worthless Continental currency, stopping veterans from reaping tangible rewards
for their service. Undoubtedly the most important result of the
black enlistments was an increase in the free Negro population
and a consequent weakening of the slave system in Rhode Island.[50]

Postwar Rhode Island was still uneasy with slavery. In 1784,
the legislature passed an act declaring that children born of slave
mothers after March 1 would be free. The legislature in 1787
passed an act prohibiting Rhode Island participation in the slave
trade:

Whereas the trade to Africa for slaves, and the transportation and selling of
them into other countries is inconsistent with justice, and the principles
of humanity, as well as the laws of nature, and that more enlightened and
civilized sense of freedom which has of late prevailed: and whereas, the
General Congress of the United States in the year 1774 taking the said
trade into consideration, agreed and resolved as follows: "That we will
neither import nor purchase any slaves imported after the first day of
December next; after which time we will wholly discontinue the slave
trade, and will neither be concerned in it ourselves, nor will we hire our
vessels or sell our commodities or manufacturers to those that are."

Nevertheless, forgetful of the danger which then impended and inat-
tentive to the principles of just and sound policy manifested in the aforesaid resolution, a renewal of the African trade for slaves has been entered
by divers inhabitants of this state; for the prevention whereof.

Be it enacted by this General Assembly, and by the authority thereof
it is enacted, that no citizen of this state, or other person residing within the same, shall for himself or any other person whatsoever either as
master, factor, or owner of any vessel, directly or indirectly import or
transport, buy or sell, or receive on board their vessel with intent to

cause to be imported or transported from their native country, any of
the natives or inhabitants of any state or kingdom in that part of the
world called Africa, as slaves, or without their voluntary consent.

And be it further enacted by the authority aforesaid, that every citizen,
inhabitant, or resident, as aforesaid, who shall import or transport, or
cause to be imported or transport, any of the said inhabitants of Africa,
contrary to the true intent and meaning of this act, and be thereof law-
fully convicted shall forfeit the sum of one hundred pounds, lawful money,
for every person by him or them so imported or transported; and the sum
of one thousand pounds for every vessel by him or them employed in the
importation or transportation aforesaid, to be recovered by bill, complaint,
or information before the superior court, or either of the inferior courts
within this state; the one moiety whereof shall be paid into the general
treasury for the use of this state, the other moiety to and for the use of
the person or persons who shall prosecute for the recovery of the same.

Provided, nevertheless that this act do not extend to vessels which are
already sailed, their owners, factors . . . for and during their present voyage

So it was to end, that which had begun as a means of substitut-
ing cheap slaves for dear servants. It would take another generation before the last of those who were slaves before 1784 would
either be manumitted or disappear from the Providence census
rolls. And masters in Rhode Island found one loophole in the
law to their advantage, as Jonathan Edwards noted in a letter to
former master turned abolitionist Moses Brown:

Dear Sir. . . . I enclose a copy of the late act of Assembly concerning the
slave trade. I am mortified as I dare say you will be, that the bill was so
mutilated in the upper house. You will find there is nothing in this law,
to prevent the exportation of slaves, and of servants born since March 1,
1784. I expect that now the poor creatures will be carried out in ship-
loads. I have heard since the passing of this law, of one man employed in
purchasing Negroes for exportation. The lower house were not pleased
with the law as it now stands; . . . inform yourself of any facts relating
to the exporting of slaves or of children born since March 1st 1784
from this state.[52]

The problem of which Edwards informed Brown in 1788 was
a difficult one for New England slaves freed under gradual emancipation statutes. Connecticut slave James Mars, freed by similar
legislation but forced to be a servant until his mid-twenties,

credited the interference of antislavery advocates with preventing his master from selling him South.[53]

If the 1790 census did not severely underenumerate the black population, Rhode Island's gradual emancipation act brought both emancipation and the exile of the soon to be manumitted feared by Jonathan Edwards. By 1790, only 46 blacks were listed as slaves in Providence. The total black population had fallen from its 1774 level of 303 to 276. Seventy-four blacks in 1790 lived in black-headed households. The others, slave and free, lived in white-headed households. Independent black households were small, none having over 6 members.[54]

Black life in colonial Providence and other parts of New England lacked many of the elements usually found in modern Afro-American communities. Providence blacks constituted a subgroup within the larger society; they had social and cultural practices that brought them together and to some extent differentiated them from whites; there was some group consciousness. None of this should be underestimated. Yet the relationships among blacks in colonial Providence were not what they would later become. The group consciousness, the realization that the larger society had defined and limited them as a group and that they would have to develop group strategies to address their circumstances, was still underdeveloped for many reasons. The most important of these reasons is that Providence blacks were slaves in a society with a premodern social structure for both blacks and whites. That meant two things. First, the rules and customs of one's household, and the slave despite his lowly status was part of the master's household, were critical in determining the day-to-day course of one's life, at least as critical as one's group identity. Although the New England slave associated with those outside his owner's household, the household nonetheless exercised a tremendous influence over the slave's associates. It was particularly influential in causing the slave to have close relationships with whites and Indians. Blacks and Narragansetts married because they worked next to each other on the dairy farms in southern Rhode Island. That is also the reason an Irish servant was included in Venture Smith's escape effort. It does not require much exercise of the historical imagination to see that the constant colonial refrain about "boys and Negroes" reflected a situation where white apprentices and the slaves they worked with together sought temporary relief from the toils that their masters imposed. Nor were close relations between slaves and servants the only interracial relationships that the household fostered. Relations between masters and slaves could be quite close. Some masters felt a responsibility for the religious and sometimes the secular instruction of their slaves. Some became the patrons of those they manumitted, continuing their contact after freedom. Even the African Governors' elections were influenced by household relations as owners became the campaign managers of their slaves, ensuring the votes of other slaves in the household, and doubtless used their relationships with other masters to ensure that slaves in other households supported their candidates.

The other reason that Providence's premodern social structure and culture affected black group consciousness was that colonial Providence was a society with strong class distinctions that few seriously challenged. This does not mean that black slaves or white servants were necessarily content. Many were not. Some ran away; others devised different strategies to attain freedom. Nor does it mean that some masters might not free a slave or servant and even help that person attain a degree of prosperity. Some did. What it does mean is that colonial Providence and the rest of colonial New England was comfortable with the idea of different classes with varying rights under the social order. In such a society there is less of a tendency among the lower classes for group strategies of social advancement to emerge. Political organizations do not recruit from among those on the bottom of the social pyramid by promising to better the conditions of subordinate classes. People seek to better their circumstances, but they do so as individuals, frequently with the patronage of those members of the upper classes whose households they have served in. Under those conditions the kind of racial frictions that have been associated with different racial groups competing for status occur less often. In colonial New England the clear acceptance of white as well as black servitude with little attempt to differentiate or elevate the former group caused that society to be less concerned with racial differences among the subordinate classes than it might have been.

All available evidence indicates that life for white servants in Providence was as difficult as life for black slaves. One advertisement for a runaway white apprentice shows how harsh life could be for white servants. The April 7, 1764, edition of the *Providence Gazette* ran an advertisement for Robert Bevlin, an eighteen-year-old escaped apprentice. The cause for Bevlin's escape was that he had been sentenced to be branded and have his ears cropped for some unspecified offense. Another advertisement showed the lowly condition of white servants. The October 15, 1768, *Gazette* ran an appeal from the master of a fifteen-year-old English apprentice. The apprentice had been threatened with sale to a man-of-war. The master promised to reconsider the sale if the boy returned.[55]

For poor whites, the possibility of being reduced to bondage was always present. In 1741, the Providence town council passed legislation that bound out the children of the poor as apprentices. In Newport in 1761, two white women, Julian Welford and Christina Renshen, were convicted of theft. Not having enough money to make restitution, they were sold to compensate their victim.[56]

White servants often had little reason to distinguish between themselves and slaves. Slaves who saw white servants bought and sold and saw that their desire to escape bondage frequently matched that of their own had little reason to see much difference between lower-class whites and themselves. This was not an uncommon phenomenon in colonial America. Slaves, servants, and apprentices North and South associated on bases of equality. These alliances began to be discouraged in the colonial South when masters began realizing that poor whites were needed as allies of the planters. Too great a friendship between poor whites and slaves represented a threat to the social equilibrium. In the North, however, such fears were less present; hence less effort was made to separate these two groups.[57]

Because they were in a society that did little to distinguish among those of different races held in servitude, because slaves in colonial Providence sought advancement in the only way open to them, freedom for the individual and perhaps family and friends, and because of their very slave status, blacks in colonial Providence did not develop the kinds of community organizations that would begin to emerge toward the end of the eighteen century and throughout the nineteenth. It would take the independence that emerged with freedom, the development of stronger racial tensions, and the desire on the part of blacks to participate in the institutions and practices of the society that they helped create that would spur the development of group consciousness. The foundation for this group consciousness had been laid in the colonial period; the transformation from African to Afro-Yankee had occurred. The new era would forge the community.

Notes

1. Winthrop Jordan, *White over Black* (Chapel Hill: University of North Carolina Press, 1968), pp. 3-40. For one of the better accounts of anti-Irish racism in seventeenth-century British colonies, see: Richard S. Dunn, *Sugar and Slaves: The Rise of the Planter Class in the English West Indies, 1624-1713* (New York: W. W. Norton, 1972), p. 69; Edmund S. Morgan, *American Slavery, American Freedom: The Ordeal of Colonial Virginia* (New York: W. W. Norton, 1975), pp. 3-25.

2. Lorenzo Johnston Greene, *The Negro in Colonial New England* (New York: Columbia University Press, 1968), p. 63; Petition of Richard Saltonstall to Massachusetts General Court, 1645, in Elizabeth Donnan, *Documents Illustrative of the History of the Slave Trade to America*, vol. 3, pp. 6-7.

3. Greene, *Negro in Colonial New England*, p. 17.

4. Donnan, *Documents*, vol. 3, pp. 6-8, Petition of Saltonstall and Disposition; Records of Massachusetts General Court, pp. 8-9; Greene, *Negro in Colonial New England*, pp. 27-38; Donnan, *Documents*, vol. 3, p. 108, Act of the General Court, May 19, 1652.

5. William D. Johnston, *Slavery in Rhode Island, 1755-1776*, Rhode Island Historical Society Publications, vol. 2 (Providence: Rhode Island Historical Society, 1894), pp. 114-15.

6. Ibid., p. 123; William B. Weeden, *Early Rhode Island* (New York: Grafton Press, 1910).

7. Johnston, *Slavery in Rhode Island*, p. 123. Italics added.

8. Ibid., p. 124.

9. Ibid., p. 126.

10. Ibid., p. 127.

11. Weeden, *Early Rhode Island*, pp. 151-52.

12. Ibid. For a detailed discussion of urban slavery, see Richard C.

Wade, *Slavery in the Cities* (New York: Oxford University Press, 1964).

13. Greene, *Negro in Colonial New England*, p. 74; *Census of the Inhabitants of the Colony of Rhode Island, 1774* (Providence: Knowles, Anthony & Co., 1858), pp. 38-53.

14. Donnan, *Documents*, vol. 3, p. 8.

15. *Records of the Boston Selectmen, 1754-1763* (Boston, 1887), p. 109; John R. Bartlett, *Records of the Colony of Rhode Island*, vol. 5, (Providence, 1860), p. 340; Bernard C. Steiner, *History of Slavery in Connecticut* (Baltimore: Johns Hopkins, 1893), pp. 13, 40.

16. Horatio Rogers, ed., *The Early Records of the Town of Providence*, vol. 2 (Providence, 1893), p. 45; Bartlett, *Records of the Colony of Rhode Island*, vol. 3, p. 492, vol. 4, p. 50; Johnston, *Slavery in Rhode Island*, pp. 136-37.

17. *Boston Selectmen*, August 12, 1761, p. 7. Italics added.

18. *Providence Gazette*, September 1, 1770.

19. *Boston Gazette*, November 11, 1765.

20. C. C. Goen, *The Works of Jonathan Edwards—The Great Awakening* (New Haven: Yale University Press, 1972), p. 159.

21. Ibid.

22. Belknap Papers, *Massachusetts Historical Collections*, Fifth Series, vol. 3, p. 383.

23. *Boston Marriages, 1700-1751* (Boston, 1889).

24. Greene, *Negro in Colonial New England*, p. 202.

25. *Census of the Inhabitants of the Colony of Rhode Island, 1774* (Providence: Knowles, Anthony & Co., 1858); Greene, *Negro in Colonial New England*, p. 202; *Heads of Families—First Census—1790 Rhode Island* (Washington, D.C.: Government Printing Office, 1908).

26. William J. Brown, *The Life of William J. Brown* (Providence: H. H. Brown, 1883), pp. 7-10; Weeden, *Early Rhode Island*, p. 135.

27. Brown, *Life of Brown*, p. 10.

28. Ibid., p. 10; Orville H. Platt, "Negro Governors," *New Haven Colony Historical Society Papers* 6, (1900), pp. 315-335; Greene, *Negro in Colonial New England*, p. 225. For a discussion of practices similar to the African Governors' in Spain and Latin America, see Roger Bastide, *African Civilizations in the New World* (New York: Harper and Row, 1971), p. 182. For a recent examination of the African Governors' elections that details their importance in Afro-American culture, see Joseph P. Reidy, "Negro Election Day and Black Community Life in New England, 1750-1850," *Marxist Perspectives* 1, no. 3 (1978): 102-17.

29. Frances McDougall, *Memoirs of Eleanor Eldridge* (Providence: B. T. Albro, 1839), pp. 34-35; Brown, *Life of Brown*, p. 13.

30. Platt, "Negro Governors," pp. 315-35; Brown, *Life of Brown*, p. 10.

31. Petition to Thomas Gage, *Massachusetts Historical Collections*, vol. 3.

32. Johnston, *Slavery in Rhode Island*, p. 115.

33. Ibid.; *Providence Gazette*, April 7, 1764; Bartlett, *Records of the Colony of Rhode Island*, vol. 9, pp. 96-97.

34. Venture Smith, *A Narrative of the Life and Adventures of Venture, A Native of Africa* (Middletown, Conn.: J. S. Stewart, 1897), pp. 14, 16-1

35. Ibid., p. 17.

36. Ibid., pp. 21-22.

37. Ibid.

38. Ibid.

39. *Providence Gazette*, November 6, 1779; Johnston, *Slavery in Rhode Island*, p. 127.

40. *Providence Gazette*, April 23, 30, May 7, 14, 21, July 9, 1763.

41. Ibid., July 22, 1769.

42. Ibid., August 25, 1770.

43. *Rhode Island Census, 1774; Providence Records*, vol. 4, p. 72; Bartlett, *Records of the Colony of Rhode Island*, vol. 4, pp. 415-16; Caroline Hazard, *College Tom: A Study of Life in Narragansett in the XVIIIth Century* (Boston: Houghton Mifflin, 1893), p. 46.

44. Greene, *Negro in Colonial New England*, pp. 291, 303; Howard M. Chapin, *A List of Rhode Island Soldiers and Sailors in the Old French and Indian War* (Providence, 1818), p. 104.

45. *Records of Boston Selectmen, 1754-1763* (Boston: 1887); Johnson, *Slavery in Rhode Island*, p. 141.

46. *Moses Brown Manumission Papers*, Probate Wills Books, p. 73, Moses Brown Papers, Rhode Island Historical Society.

47. Bartlett, *Records of the Colony of Rhode Island*, vol. 8, pp. 359-61; Lorenzo J. Greene, "Some Observations on the Black Regiment of Rhode Island in the American Revolution" *Journal of Negro History* 37 (April 1952): 142-72; Sidney S. Rider, *An Historical Inquiry Concerning the Attempt to Raise a Regiment of Slaves by Rhode Island* (Providence: Rhode Island Historical Society, 1880), pp. 1-11.

48. Bartlett, *Records of the Colony of Rhode Island*, vol. 8, p. 361; Greene, "Some Observations," pp. 152-53.

49. Greene, "Some Observations," pp. 157-59; *List of Black Servicemen Compiled from the War Department Collection of Revolutionary War Records* (Washington, D.C.: National Archives and Record Service, General Services Administration, 1974).

50. Benjamin Quarles, *The Negro in the American Revolution* (Chapel Hill: University of North Carolina Press, 1961), pp. 80-82; McDougall, *Memoirs of Eleanor Eldridge*, p. 20.

51. Donnan, *Documents*, pp. 343-44.

52. Ibid., p. 345.

53. James Mars, *Life of James Mars, a Slave Born and Sold in Connecticut* (Hartford, 1868), pp. 8-9.

54. U.S. Census, 1790, (manuscript).

55. *Providence Gazette*, April 7, 1764, October 15, 1768.

56. Bartlett, *Records of the Colony of Rhode Island*, vol. 5, p. 157; Johnston, *Slavery in Rhode Island*, p. 118.

57. Henry Dorr, *The Planting and Growth of Providence* (Providence: S. S. Rider, 1882), p. 208; Morgan, *American Slavery*, pp. 333-36.

INSTITUTION
BUILDING

2

In Providence, as elsewhere in the new nation, the late eighteenth and early nineteenth centuries was an ambiguous time in American race relations and Afro-American community development. The emancipation of 1784 had brought neither immediate independence nor an instant break with the racial milieu of the slave era. For the black people of Providence, the decades following emancipation were to be a time of burgeoning consciousness and organization. Spurred on partly by a national mood that encouraged citizens to involve themselves in the governing, improvement, and maintenance of their society and partly by the exclusion of blacks from such participation, blacks in Providence began grouping together, rejecting and accepting proposals and strategies for their mutual benefit, and forging the links of a community.

The changes that came occurred because the development of a free Negro class forced white and black into new modes of behavior toward themselves and each other. The growth of the free Negro class also coincided with the improvement of the circumstances of the white laboring class. In the post-Revolutionary period, when thousands of slaves North and South were the beneficiaries of private manumissions and state emancipations, white servitude, already limited by the time of the Revolution, declined into insignificance. The late eighteenth and early nine-

teenth centuries also brought many efforts to improve the educa
tion, morals, and political participation of the white poor, as
church and school solicited the participation of a large part of
the population and as access to the ballot box became less
dependent on property qualifications.[1]

Throughout the nation, the simultaneous improvement in the
position of poor whites and the creation of a free Negro class
raised questions of the extent to which blacks would benefit
from the democratic and egalitarian currents in the new republic. In the North particularly, the question of how to treat newly freed blacks arose as the spectre of large-scale black participation in public institutions became a possibility that many
feared. How were the benefits of citizenship to be extended
to the free Negro? Should blacks be allowed to vote, serve on
juries, attend school, bear arms, become church members—in
short, possess the badges of citizenship that were being bestowe
on an ever wider portion of the population?

Initially it seemed as if the nation might choose racial equalit
for the recently freed blacks. When most states enacted their
initial legislation concerning voting requirements, they did not
specifically prohibit black suffrage. Similarly, there were no
specific restrictions against blacks holding public office or serving in the militia. These discriminations began occurring in the
late eighteenth and early nineteenth centuries. The federal gove
ment restricted the militia to white men in 1792.[2] Rhode Islan
banned voting by blacks in 1822.

It is hard to determine exactly what caused the erosion of
black rights in the early nineteenth century. In some states it
was doubtless the case that the initial drafters of state statutory
and constitutional provisions permitting blacks to serve as vote
jury members, or militiamen did so through oversight; they
failed to include the word *white* in their listing of the qualifications of freemen, perhaps feeling that that was understood. But
other evidence indicates that the lack of restrictions during this
period was an outgrowth of the liberal sentiments that the Rev
lution had nurtured. This is best seen in the voting rights issue.

In a number of states in the late eighteenth and early nineteenth centuries, free Negroes voted in sufficient numbers to be
noticed. They tended to vote for Federalist candidates, probabl

reflecting their continued patron-client ties with the upper-class whites in the Northeast. Dixon Ryan Fox has asserted that as early as 1800, black voters in New York were able to swing close elections to the Federalist party.[3] This caused the Democratic-Republican party to press for the disenfranchisement of black voters. Although this did not occur, in 1821 when property qualifications for white voters were eliminated, a new property qualification of $250 was imposed on black voters.[4] This and parallel developments in Pennsylvania, a state where blacks were thrown off the voting rolls in 1838, indicates that there was a period when the free black voter had a measure of acceptance and was later consciously disenfranchised by political forces who saw him as a threat.

In Rhode Island, the deterioration of the free Negro's legal status had occurred as he became more of a potential threat to total white control. There are indications that a few black men attained freeman status in Rhode Island before the 1822 disenfranchisement.[5] These people, unlike the New Yorkers dealt with by Fox, do not seem to have become a measurable political force. Nonetheless, the increased property holding and independence of Rhode Island blacks augured for future political significance.

Related to the erosion of black rights in the early nineteenth century were the increasing patterns of conflict between blacks and working-class whites. The abolition of slavery and the curtailment of various forms of white servitude altered the relationships between laboring blacks and whites. They were less likely to be found as servants in the same household than they were during the colonial period. They were more likely to view each other as economic competitors as the members of both groups became independent economic agents. As slaves, blacks had been guaranteed, even if they had not always desired, employment. Masters could permit their slaves to be artisans. With a substantial number of whites in temporary bondage, the slave artisan was not competing with whites for employment; often as not he was working with a white apprentice or indentured servant. Slave artisans and white servant artisans were not each other's competitors, though their respective masters may have been. While it certainly mattered to the master of a colonial household whether his particular carpenter's or blacksmith's shop received business or his competitor's did, and indirectly it affected the well-being of a slave or servant in the household also, such concerns had less of a racial dimension to them and more of the character of competition between households. The emancipation of both black slaves and white servants fostered the development of competition between the two groups as both found that it mattered who secured jobs as artisans. This new competition that formed after blacks could no longer depend on a household-centered economy to allow them access to skilled trades has caused local historians of Providence to refer to the slave era as the "golden age" of black artisans in Providence. Slavery was the time when blacks, least encumbered by white competition and restriction, were most able to work at skilled trades.[6]

White America's reaction to the evolving free Negro population in the decades following the Revolution was that of a society that at first was dealing with an anomaly and later with a significant social phenomenon. Less attention is paid to developing rules governing the behavior of anomalies than is paid to setting limits for groups that constitute major portions of a population. In a way, the evolving status of the free Negro might be likened to the differences in treatment that pilot groups (the first wave of a particular ethnic group's immigration into an area) experienced as opposed to the social reaction the larger mass of a particular ethnic group experienced.

While white Americans pondered what role they would assign to the emerging free Negro population, free blacks in the early nineteenth-century North had to answer two related sets of questions about their status and role in the evolving American Republic. The first problem confronting free Negroes was one of cultural expression. They wanted to reflect the culture that had been thrust upon them in their two-century sojourn in North America and was now theirs. Culturally American, black northerners wanted the benefits of church, school, temperance society, militia company, self-improvement society, and fraternal order. These were desired by most Americans in the early nineteenth century, and blacks were no exception; the only difference was that growing racism precluded their participation in such institutions.

Ironically, the earliest black organization to reflect black Providence's cultural adaptation to the New England milieu was a society that sought the colonization of free blacks in Africa. The Free African Union Society was founded in Newport in 1780 by free blacks who wanted to emigrate to Africa. By 1789, the Newport organization was inviting blacks in Providence to form a chapter of the society. The Newport organization's letter, addressed "To All the Africans in Providence," stressed the horrors of the slave trade and plantation slavery in the West Indies and the American South. It also noted that some benevolent whites were aiding the society in the African repatriation effort. The letter instructed Providence blacks that the Free African Union Society held meetings once every three months "to consider what can be done for our good and the good of all Africans, and in the meantime we still wait on the Lord, and are ready to do all the good we can, whether we are called to go there, or stay here." So the Newport leaders invited Providence blacks:

Therefore our sincere desire is that you would join us in this society so that we all may promote one common good—We have agreed upon certain regulations to be maintained in the Society, which you may see, and if you should fully comply and join us, you shall have part of the Officers at Providence.[7]

A group of black men in Providence responded favorably to the invitation. On September 22, 1789, they sent a letter to the Newport organization agreeing to act as a subordinate part of it. The Providence group developed an organization that included a vice-president, a moderator, six representatives, one treasurer, a deputy secretary, and a sheriff. Because mutual relief was one of the reasons for the organization's existence, the Providence group asked the Newport organization if it would be possible for indigent members who could not be relieved by the Providence organization to petition the Newport society for aid. The Newport group agreed to this request.[8]

By 1794, the Providence group began to be ambitious to be something more than a simple satellite of the Newport organization. On January 15, 1794, the Providence group asked the Newport group to help finance an expedition to Sierra Leone to ex-

amine it for Afro-American colonization. The Newport organization urged caution and indicated that it would be better if the
Newport group handled any African explorations.[9]

As the eighteenth century ended and the nineteenth century
unfolded, the African emigrationist tendencies of the Free African Union Society gave way to the highly pragmatic self-help
and mutual aid desires of Newport's African Benevolent Society
This organization, which lasted from 1807 to 1824, seems to
have been primarily concerned with burial of members, relief
of the widows of members, and establishing a school for black
children.[10]

The letters of the Free African Union Society, from both New
port and Providence, reveal the high degree of acculturation, the
transition from African to Yankee, that had occurred among the
would-be emigrants. Nowhere in the correspondence of the Free
African Union Society is there a mention of any specific African
place except the British colony of Sierra Leone as a location for
a settlement. No mention is made of any specific African group
as a people who might be compatible neighbors for the would-
be settlers. The Africa they sought to settle had become a strang
land during their sojourn in the New World and from one of thei
accounts a strange land in need of their American enlightenment

the nations in Africa, from we sprang, being in heathenish darkness and
barbarity, and are, and have been for many years, many of them, so foolish
and wicked as to sell one another into slavery, by which many millions
have either lost their lives, or been transported to a land of slavery.[11]

Other correspondence indicated how the emigration effort
would benefit not only free blacks in the United States but
would also serve as a means of uplifting African nations. Strong
Christian beliefs are indicated in the society's correspondence,
as well as a strong desire to have free blacks present a good imag
to the larger society, particularly potential white patrons. The
Free African Union Society endorsed a report of the deputies
of abolition societies, written in 1796, that among other things
called upon free blacks to

fifthly, refrain from the use of spirits . . . sixthly, avoid frolicking and
amusements that lead to expense and idleness; they beget habits of dis-

sipation and vice, and thus expose you to deserved reproach amongst
your white neighbors. Seventhly, we wish to impress upon your minds
the moral and religious necessity of having your marriages legally performed; also to have exact registers preserved of all the births and deaths
which occur in your respective families.[12]

The first black organization that developed in Rhode Island
showed that even those contemplating African settlement had
already experienced a high, perhaps overwhelming, degree of
cultural assimilation by the late eighteenth and early nineteenth
centuries. Organizations that would later develop in the nineteenth century would also reflect this assimilation, as well as
black exclusion from the institutions of the larger society.

In addition to the desire to reflect and participate in their
new culture, black northerners had to address the question of
political activism and how such would benefit the individual,
the immediate community, and the black race in America, most
of which was enslaved. This second set of questions included
such matters as how to acquire or retain access to the ballot
box, whether to press for public education for black children,
and, later on, whether to press for integrated educational facilities, the desirability of attacking Jim Crow, and overt prohibition of blacks from public facilities. Finally, these political
questions also included whether to support abolitionist movements or colonizationist and emigrationist efforts.

In some northern black communities, political protest developed simultaneously with and even prior to the formation of
institutions for separate cultural expression. One might point
to the efforts of Paul Cuffee and other eighteenth-century Massachusetts blacks to get the vote as an example of this.[13] In other
black communities, such as Providence, organizations that served
as independent vehicles of cultural expression, usually centered on
an autonomous black church, preceded political protest, or more
properly the antebellum struggle for equal rights.

The development in Providence of independent vehicles of
cultural expression by blacks was an outgrowth of the development of independent black households. Such households put
black men in positions they had never been in before. Heading
households, out from under the master's control, black men had

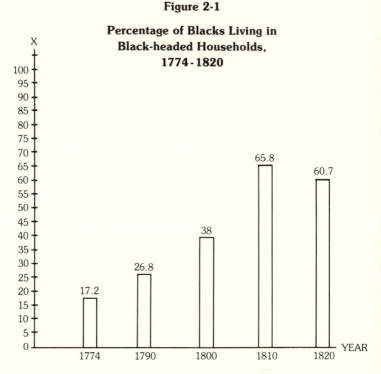

Figure 2-1

Percentage of Blacks Living in Black-headed Households, 1774-1820

to make decisions for their families on such matters as the education of their children, the religious environment of their families, and how to protect their families in an increasingly hostile
society. Moving out of the master's household was the first step
in the building of black institutions.

A person who had left Providence prior to Rhode Island's
gradual emancipation act of 1784 and had returned by 1790
would not have found the situation of Providence's black residents greatly altered. To be sure, by 1790 slaves were a distinct
minority of the enumerated black population; only 44 of the
276 blacks listed in the census were slaves. It was also true by
1790 that 26.8 percent of Providence's Afro-Americans lived
in black-headed households, up 9.6 percentage points from the
17.2 percent of the 1774 census (see figure 2-1). The majority
of blacks in 1790 lived in white-headed households, performing the tasks that their former master desired.[14]

The preemancipation bonds between former slave and former master continued not only in the dwelling places of the newly freed but in social processes as well. Control of religion, education of the young, and even the interaction of black people with each other were heavily influenced by the former master.[15]

Blacks in Providence's polydenominational society either attended the churches of their masters or those of other whites. William J. Brown, whose family had been slaves and servants of Moses Brown, recalled that he attended Providence's First Baptist Church, even though Moses Brown belonged to the Society of Friends. Sharing memories of his early nineteenth-century childhood, Brown recalled the caste division within the First Baptist Church, telling us a bit about black education and social stratification in a white church:

The Sabbath School was something new, and the people had many conjectures about it. At the proper time we left home, and arrived at school. I remember being much pleased with my nice clothes and still more so, as I saw so many boys and girls of all sizes at the school, all dressed so nice and clean, also some beautiful ladies and gentlemen. I thought it one of the most charming sights I ever beheld. Soon the school commenced, classes were made up and whilst I was trying to see everybody and hear everything that was said, someone tapped me on the shoulder. . . . Then she got some cards and heard me say the alphabet. As I had learned a good part of them from my brothers and sisters, I was a good hand in repeating the alphabet. The lady came soon after and brought some beautiful cards, which pleased me much, and asked me to come next Sunday. I told her I would. After the school closed, I went to the First Baptist Church in company with Miss Wescott climbing up three or four pairs of stairs to where the colored people sat.[16]

He later noted:

The largest number [of blacks], however, were Baptists, belonged to the First Baptist Church, but many attended no church at all, because they said they were opposed to going to churches and sitting in pigeon holes, as all the churches at that time had some obscure place for colored people to sit in.[17]

Brown's passages give two pictures of the First Baptist Church. On one hand, we see an integrated Sunday school providing

white and black children with something of a rudimentary educ
tion, doubtless a continuation of the Puritan tradition that man
dated education for all, ensuring the ability to read the Bible. O
the other, church services were segregated, with blacks relegated
to the least desirable positions in a congregation. As was the cas
during slavery, a black person might be accorded full membersh
despite consignment to a caste seat. William J. Brown's mother,
for instance, was a full member of the First Baptist Church.[18]

Education for black children in the first decades following th
1784 emancipation was a continuation of the patterns that
existed during slavery. Black children's education depended on
their relationship to white people. A church whose Sunday sch
admitted black children, a master who permitted a servant child
to listen to his child's tutor or receive his child's lessons second-
hand, these were largely responsible for much of the literacy th
existed among Providence blacks. One exception seems to have
been a school, run by Quaker educator John Lawton, which ad
mitted black and white in the late eighteenth century. Its cost
was, however, prohibitive for most blacks, and it is probable
that mostly blacks connected with white Quaker families went
to this school.[19]

One reason that whites had such a large influence over black
education was that black children frequently lived in white hou
holds. Poor black families often apprenticed their children to
white households, hoping that money and training would be th
result of such associations. Eleanor Eldridge and William J. Bro
both, for a time, lived as servants in white households.[20] Brown
described the agreement worked out between his father and a
Captain Childs concerning his becoming a servant:

Captain Childs took a great liking to me, and wanted me to live with
him. Father said he was willing, provided he would give me victuals
and clothing, and schooling one half each day which he consented to
do, but I was to sleep at home. I went and liked it very well. The Captain
and his wife were very fine people. . . . My work was very light such as
going on errands, etc.[21]

If the census of 1820 can serve as an indication, such arrang
ments were common. That census shows 20 percent of black
children under fourteen living in white-headed households. Of

the forty-two white households that had black children under age fourteen listed with them, twenty-two, or 52 percent, showed black children alone with no black adults, indicating that these households did not have whole black families, just children.[22] This meant strong white control over the black child's development.

As the nineteenth century unfolded, the number of independent black households increased (see figure 2-1). Finding housing and meeting the needs of their families for space and safety was a formidable task for the heads of black families in early nineteenth-century Providence. Developing prejudice, coupled with the poverty of most black families, limited housing selections. Popular prejudice prevented black families from moving into anything larger than two-room dwellings.[23] As in other cities, blacks were forced to live in high-vice and high-crime areas, neighborhoods populated by toughs, brawling sailors, prostitutes, and tormenting urchins.

One of the first battles of the black population in Providence was the fight to maintain the Christian values, courtesies, trappings of respectability, and civility acquired during their Rhode Island sojourn. Brown described the problems his family encountered trying to secure adequate lodging while keeping their social distance from the undesirable classes:

I have remarked that father moved into a house called Red Lion. This name was given to the house because of its former occupants, which did not bear a very good character. Providence being a commercial place always having a large amount of shipping in port, consequently there was a large supply of sailors who could be seen at all times in the day. In this locality there were a large number of sailor boarding houses to accommodate them: and for their convenience there were many grog shops to refresh themselves in; and their numerous attractions enticing many lewd females. The house which my father rented being located in the south part of the town, near the water was a very desirable location for such characters, hence it received the name of Red Lion. . . . When we first moved in we occupied the upper rooms, until the family below could vacate their rooms, which was some six months after we moved in. Two rooms was considered quite a genteel tenement in those days for a family of six, especially if they were colored, the prevailing opinion being that they had no business with a larger house than one or two rooms. The family occupying the lower floor of our house were considered the upper crust of the colored population, Mr. Thomas Reed by name, by trade a barber, and kept a fashionable shaving salon. They occupied the whole house, using the upstairs as a genteel boarding house. He did not accommodate sailors and thus regained the reputation of the house, which had been previously occupied and patronized by the lower classes.[24]

Unlike Thomas Reed, many Negroes in early nineteenth-century Providence could not banish the city's more rowdy elements from their midst; they often found themselves in conflict with the more boisterous denizens of the waterfront communities that they inhabited. Harassment by rowdies was a constant problem for black people in Providence. Whole neighborhoods became gauntlets for blacks in Providence, areas where there was an ever-present fear of being set upon by criminals. Little protection was offered to black people by the authorities, as Brown observed:

Colored people had little or no protection from the law at those times unless they resided with some white gentlemen that would take up their case for them. If you were well dressed they would insult you for that, and if you were ragged you would surely be insulted for being so; be as peaceable as you could be there was no shield for you. One day I was going [to the African Union Meeting House]. . . . Two colored ladies were close behind us followed by two white men who ordered them off the sidewalk or they would kick them off. The females fearing they would do so, went out into the street and walked until they came on the walk near us. The men then ordered us off. My companion gave me the lamp and grappled with one of the men, who being a tall strong man, threw him into the gangway where he fell.

One tall well dressed man said to the people that rounded us, take these niggers to jail for I have seen enough of their actions today. Without further information we were seized, and would have been dragged off to prison and locked up, had it not been for the timely appearances of Mr. Joseph Balch who came out of his apothecary shop, being well acquainted with us both. He exclaimed, hold on, "what are you going to do with these boys?" and this would-be somebody said "we are going to take them to prison. I have seen enough of their actions today." Mr. Balch replied, "no, you won't, I know both of them, they are nice boys." . . . We went on and the crowd dispersed.[25]

Tensions developed from relatively minor street encounters.
Two race riots occurred in Providence as a result of the conflicts
between blacks trying to develop family stability and respectability and lower-class whites seeking to gain status by fighting
their only socially acceptable target, blacks. The Hardscrabble
riot of 1824 and the Olney Street riot of 1831 were major indi-
cators of the conflict between these two groups. The Hardscrabble
riot of October 18, 1824, started amid an atmosphere of increased
white apprehension over the black presence in Providence, particularly in the Hardscrabble area in the northwestern part of the
city. During that month, the *Providence Gazette* ran an editorial
advocating colonization of blacks in Haiti. The editorial especially condemned recent black migrants to Providence, declaring
them to be responsible for a large amount of crime and mis-
chief.[26]

Hardscrabble was a poor neighborhood in the 1820s. Its cheap
rent attracted large numbers of black people, as Brown tells us:

In the northwest part of the city was a place called Addison Hollow, but
was nick-named Hardscrabble. A great many colored people purchased
land there, because it was some distance from town and hence quite cheap.
They put up small houses for themselves and earned their living in various
ways. . . . Some men did jobs of gardening and farming.[27]

The cheap rents also attracted black and white undesirables.
Brown further describes the population of Hardscrabble:

A man named Addison built houses, and rented to anyone who would
give him his price. As he rented cheap, people of bad character hired of
him, and these drew a class of bad men and women, so that the good
were continually being molested, having no protection.[28]

The cheap rents and the growing vice atmosphere attracted
undesirables from outside Rhode Island who sought to escape
police harassment. These people added to the tribulations of
the poor working-class black families forced to live in the Hardscrabble area because of economic circumstances. Tensions grew
among Hardscrabble residents and between Hardscrabble residents and whites living in other areas of Providence.

On the evening of October 18, 1824, a white mob, incensed by the failure of blacks in the Hardscrabble area to get off the sidewalk when approached by whites, began forming in northwestern Providence.[29] Approximately forty members of the mob gathered in front of the house of a black resident of Hardscrabble, Henry T. Wheeler. The downstairs of Wheeler's house was a dance hall. Wheeler lived in the upstairs of the dwelling. The mob was armed with clubs, and there were between three and six axes in the mob's possession. The group began the destruction of Wheeler's house. Midway through that process they left Wheeler's house to attack other dwellings. Later on that night, between fifty and sixty people returned to complete the razing of Wheeler property. The mob carried lamps on the moonless night and accomplished their purpose with clubs and by passing the small number of axes around to various members of the crowd.[30] Some twenty houses were destroyed.

The mob's actions were met with resistance by the residents of Hardscrabble. One of the people present in the crowd and later charged with riot for his actions in the Hardscrabble activities, Oliver Cummins, was grazed in the mouth with a bullet shot by an unidentified resident of Hardscrabble. Cummins appears to have been guarding the mob against attack by Hardscrabble residents. He, and presumably some of the others armed with clubs was standing guard waiting for a black attack on the mob that was destroying the neighborhood.[31]

Oliver Cummins, Nathaniel Metcalf, Gilbert Humes, and Arthur Farrier were brought to trial for their roles in the Hardscrabble riot. Their trials gave defense attorneys opportunities to justify the defendants' actions by declaring Hardscrabble and its inhabitants to be public nuisances. Defense attorney Joseph L. Tilinghast in his closing statement at Oliver Cummins's trial said

Gentlemen of the jury,—The renowned city of Hardscrabble lies buried in its magnificent ruins! Like the ancient Babylon it has fallen with all its graven images, its tables of impure oblation, its idolatrous rights and sacrifices. . . . Hardscrabble! The origin of this name I cannot pretend to trace. . . .

It is much to be regretted that among the thirty or forty witnesses the Attorney General has examined, some of them have not explained the

etymology of this name. Perhaps after all it is only meant as descriptive
of the *shuffling* which is there practised in the graceful evolutions of the
dance, or the zig zag movements of Pomp and Phillis, when engaged in
treading the minuet de la cour! But be that as it may, we must all agree
the destruction of this place is a benefit to the morals of the community.[32]

Of the defendants who came to trial, Oliver Cummins and Gilbert Humes were declared not guilty, Nathaniel Metcalf was
found guilty, and the jury in Arthur Farrier's case declared
that he was factually though not legally guilty. A major portion
of the defense argument was that the defendants had done a
public service by removing a rowdy element from Providence.

But the mob did not differentiate between guilty and innocent,
respectable families and social deviants, or the hard-working and
the criminals. However much apologists for the mob would point
to the undesirables whose activities were curtailed by the riot, the
riot started because whites were angry at the failure of blacks to
show deference to them; and the homes of hard-working blacks
as well as dance halls were pulled down. One of these hard-working
family men was Christopher Hill, a widower with three children
who supported himself by odd jobs, frequently woodcutting. His
house was torn down and his furniture taken by the mob, later
to be sold in neighboring Pawtucket. He and his children spent
the ensuing winter in his cellar, using the roof that had survived
the destruction to cover the opening in the ground. Neighbors
and white philanthropists offered him other dwellings, but he
and his children stayed in the cellar. In the spring of 1825, he and
his children went to Liberia.[33]

In 1831, a similar riot occurred on Olney Street. Like the Hardscrabble area, the west end of Olney Street was populated by a
mixed lot of hard-working, law-abiding, poor black families and
prostitutes and criminals. Olney Street, located in the northern
part of Providence, was a gathering place for the sailors who put
into Providence's port. Bars, dance halls, and houses of prostitution vied with each other for the opportunity to separate the sea-
man from his money. Black sailors and white sailors, sometimes
integrated and sometimes separated, moved from tavern to dance
hall to house of prostitution, often drunk and frequently ready to
brawl.

On September 21, 1831, Providence blacks once again endure assault on their property and person during the course of an anti black riot. According to one account, the riot's catalyst was a black man called Rattler. The Rattler, as this account related it, left the boardinghouse of a man identified as "Uncle Jimmie." Brown tells us about "Uncle Jimmie's":

After the sailors had stayed at Uncle Jimmie's boarding house long enough to be stripped of nearly all their money by Uncle Jimmie and his wife, and the females which hung around there, they would be suffered to stroll up to Olney Street to spend the rest of their money.[34]

The Rattler went to a dance hall frequented by sailors. Drunk or naturally gauche, the Rattler ran amok in the dance hall "dancing, running against one man and pushing against another." Five men decided to fight the Rattler, but he proved too much for the group, throwing one man against the bar, another across the room of the dance hall, butting the heads of the others against the walls of the room. Needless to say, the Rattler's actions broke up the dance hall, spilling out onto Olney Street.[35]

Groups of white and black seamen began fighting. That first night, September 21, the black sailors drove the white sailors from Olney Street. The next night a white mob returned to avenge the previous night's defeat. A black resident of Olney Street fired on the mob, and one of the mob's members was killed. The mob succeeded in destroying two houses of blacks that night. They came back a third night, buttressed by additional antiblack recruits from Providence and the other towns. They warned some of the working-class blacks on Olney Street to leave and then proceeded to tear up the homes of the Olney Street residents.[36]

As an inducement to encourage others to join the riot, which was not completely finished until September 24, rioters announced that not only would there be booty from the destroyed homes of Olney Street residents, but banks and businesses in the area could be looted as well. Civil authorities, somewhat less than enthusiastic about this prospect, decided that the time had come to squelch the riot. The sheriff and the governor appealed to the mob to disperse; their efforts failed. On September 23, twenty-five militiamen were routed by the rioters. The disturbances continued. Finally, on September 24 two militia companies were sent in to quell the riot. A justice of the peace read a dispersal order; the mob persisted, pelting justice and militiamen with stones. The soldiers opened fire, killing four mob members and the riot.[37]

The Hardscrabble and Olney Street riots were extreme examples of forces that were shaping a separate and inferior place in Providence society for blacks. In day-to-day conflicts with rowdy whites or in major riots, Providence blacks found the law reluctant to extend its protection to them. In business dealings blacks were swindled out of money, labor, and property, while the law provided little redress. Both Eleanor Eldridge and Noah Brown, William Brown's father, were cheated out of property by whites with the acquiescence of legal officials. The extremity of the Hardscrabble riot situation was probably a contributing factor to the emigration of thirty-two blacks from Rhode Island to Africa in 1826, eighteen months after the riot. They sailed with Newport Gardiner of the Free African Union Society, with the financial backing of the American Colonization Society. They were the only group of blacks to have left Rhode Island for Liberia under the auspices of the Colonization Society.[38]

Encountering these problems was part of the maturation process for blacks in Providence. In separate households, removed from the protection that former masters bestowed, either out of kindliness or a desire to preserve their property, blacks in Providence encountered hostilities and learned that their only protection lay in united efforts.

One of the earliest of these efforts was the organizing of the African Union Meeting House, Providence's first black church. Formed in 1819, the African Union Meeting House's formation reflected both the older paternalism of the more enlightened master as well as early nineteenth-century stirrings of black consciousness. Moses Brown, whose career evolved from slaveholder, to abolitionist, to colonizationist, and finally to advocate for the betterment of the conditions of free blacks in Providence, was one of the prime movers in the white community for the establishment of a black church. Moses Brown purchased the land on which the church was built, and the meeting for the establishment of the African Union Meeting House was held in Providence's First Baptist Church. The white clergymen of Providence invited prominent members of the black community to the meeting to discuss the formation of a black church, partly to get black members out of white congregations, partly to minister to the large number of blacks in Providence who were not church members because they would not abide segregated pews.[39]

The founding of the African Union Meeting House also demon strated the new concerns of independent black heads of households and the development of property holding and wealth-based status differentiation among blacks. "The land . . . Moses Brown paid two hundred dollars . . . and donated to the congregation was sold to him by a black man, George McCarty."[40] Of the $2,200 raised for the founding of the African Union Meet ing House, $800 came from the black community.[41]

The community, appointed at the organizational meeting held at the First Baptist Church, also reflected the growing independence and status of some blacks in Providence. The initial committee consisted of Warwick Sweetland, Abraham Gibb George McCarty, George J. Smith, George C. Willis, Joshua Weeks, Derry Williams, Hodge Congdon, Nathaniel Paul, Henry Taber, Peter Waters, and Thomas Graham. Later James Harris, Thomas Thompson, George W. Barrett, Henry Greene, Stephen Wolmsly, and Asa C. Godsbury were added to the group.[42]

An examination of this committee shows the dominance of the independent household head and the black parent. The census of 1820 reveals most of these men to be heads of households with children and young adults living in them. Only Nathaniel Paul, George J. Smith, Derry Williams, Peter Waters, George Barrett, and Asa Goldsbury were not listed as heads of households that included children.[43] William J. Brown revealed that Nathaniel Paul was a minister who was sent around New England by the Providence black community to raise money for the African Union Meeting House.[44] Asa C. Goldsbury, described by Brown as "an octoroon, and many people took him to be white," was from the Baptist Church of Christ in Woburn, Massachusetts, and new to Providence in 1819 when the church was founded.[45]

The African Union Meeting House's organization reveals the

links the family-heading black men of the church committee had to the white philanthropists of Providence. The opening of the church saw the considerable participation of many of the white friends of black betterment in Providence. A parade to the new church building included Quakers and other whites who had aided in the establishment of the black church. The opening address was delivered by the Reverend Henry Jackson, a white minister. Benjamin C. Wade, a white music instructor, brought the previously established African choir into the African Union Meeting House, as the author of *A Short History of the African Union Meeting House* mentioned:

The singing on this occasion was admirably performed by the African choir, under the direction of Mr. Benjamin C. Wade; a young gentlemen who had for some time past distinguished himself as their sincere friend, by his prudent and judicious counsel and unwearied exertions to improve them in sacred musick, morals and piety. There is reason to believe much good has resulted from his labors, which it is hoped will tend to cheer and encourage him in future life.[46]

White ministers of the various denominations found in Providence conducted services at the African Union Meeting House as that church's official history described:

Meetings after this period were constantly held in this room on Lord's day evenings and frequently on the sabbath and during the week. The Reverend Clergy, of this and the neighboring towns, officiated on these occasions. The Society of Friends have held only one meeting in the house. This is deeply regretted. It is sincerely wished, that they will often make it convenient to favor the people of colour with their advice and instruction.[47]

The presence of white clergy and laymen sympathetic to the African Union Meeting House was not the only way that the church reflected black-white ties. The very organization of the church strongly echoed the values of colonial and early national Providence. The church was to be interdenominational, reflecting Rhode Island's tradition of religious toleration, a tradition that caused Providence to have many denominations. Among the white churches that helped in the formation of the African Union Meeting House, the Baptist, Congregationalist, and Methodist denominations were represented.[48] These denominations also provided the initial membership from among their black parishioners.

The African Union Meeting House reflected emerging status within Providence's black community. Lacking funds to complete the church building, the governing committee decided to sell pews to raise money, a common practice in early America; it was a normal occurrence for prominent families to hold a family pew. Pews in the African Union Meeting House were reserved for those blacks able to buy them, visitors, and white friends of the African Union Meeting House. The price of a pew seemed to be around twenty dollars, and with the purchase of a pew one got to vote on church affairs. This privilege was extended to women as well as men who bought pews.[49]

One of the purposes of the African Union Meeting House, perhaps the one that most concerned the family men who were present at the church's genesis, was to further the education of black children. The educational situation for black children was haphazard. From the beginning, it was planned that the African Union Meeting House would house a school for black children. This school was to educate the major portion of black children in Providence before the common school system in the 1830s recognized its responsibilities in the instruction of black children. This school was also to be a focal point of black response to racism—racism that hurt their children and was reflected by the white teachers who were hired.

An integral part of the church from the African Union Meeting House's inception, the school connected to the church was heavily influenced by the Quaker supporters of the African Union Meeting House. During the planning of school policy, the Quakers urged the adoption of the Lancasterian system of teaching for the black school. Originated by English Quakers, the Lancasterian plan was a popular method for the education of the children of the poor and was found wherever members of the Society of Friends were instrumental in setting up a system. A regimented system, the method emphasized the use of student monitors to teach younger children.[50]

The school opened with a white teacher, Mr. Ormsbee, as its first master. It filled a strongly felt need. Although it charged its pupils $1.50 a quarter for tuition and despite its cramped housing in the vestry of the African Union Meeting House, 125 students enrolled in the school in its first year. A harsh disciplinarian who frequently inflicted corporal punishment on his pupils, Ormsbee left after a year of teaching. The school was closed for a year and a half after that because it was difficult for the school to find teachers. There were few blacks at the time capable of teaching school, and whites were reluctant to teach at black schools. Afterward the school obtained two black teachers, Asa Goldsbury and Jacob Perry, both of whom doubled as preachers in the church.[51]

The school partially answered the black community's need for education, but it also presented the black community with many difficulties. Teachers were hard to find, and the school seems to have secured people who were passing through Providence on their way elsewhere. William Brown noted that one of his white teachers made a point of not recognizing his pupils on the street; in fact, in class he gave this warning: "When you meet me on the street, don't look towards me, or speak to me; if you do, I will flog you the first chance I get."[52]

Another problem with the African Union Meeting House School was that students or their parents had to pay, which added to the haphazard nature of education for the children attending the school. Thus a student's education would be interrupted by both the comings and goings of teachers and the necessity of dropping out for lack of funds. In 1828 as part of its general establishment of common schools, Rhode Island recognized its responsibilities in the education of Providence's black children by opening the Meeting Street School. Another school, the Pond Street School, was opened in 1837. State law dictated that funds for education were to be distributed to each town in proportion to the white population under fifteen years of age and the black population under ten. With the exception of a few rural areas, Rhode Island maintained a dual school system until 1865.[53]

The same desire for respectability that motivated the founding of the African Union Meeting House was present in the founding of other organizations that worked for the uplifting of the black people of Providence. Growing out of the church and school, the black youth of Providence formed a self-improvement society. A chapter of the Prince Hall Masons was formed. This organization, which paralleled the white Mason group, was first started in Massachusetts, and chapters spread throughout the North. In 1832, moreover, the Providence black population got involved in a movement that was to have nationwide support and opposition for many decades following: temperance.[54]

The Providence Temperance Society was founded by the Reverend John Lewis. His career in Providence was typical of many other itinerant black ministers in that city. There was a strong desire for self-improvement among the adult blacks of Providence. The schools for their children did not satisfy their own desires for learning, so a number of black ministers who passed through Providence, as well as sympathetic whites, opened night academies for blacks.[55]

Lewis had opened one such academy in 1836. Perhaps because of the desire of the black population to put a considerable distance between themselves and the rowdy elements they were forced to dwell among, Lewis was able to get two hundred members of Providence's black community to take the pledge for temperance.[56] He made Providence a center of black temperance and in 1836 he held a Convention of People of Color for the Promotion of Temperance in New England.[57] Lewis managed to gather black and sympathetic white delegates from all over New England. The Reverend Amos Gerry Beman, a black leader then from Hartford and later active in New Haven, was a delegate. William Lloyd Garrison lent support to the endeavor by his presence. The convention's resolves forswore all intoxicating beverages and mentioned that intemperance was responsible for pauperism and crime.[58]

In his address to the convention, the Reverend John Lewis linked the causes of temperance and the uplift of the black race. He said that while blacks were less prone to intemperance than whites, that nonetheless it worked to "impoverish our pockets, injure our health, mar our character, deprave our morals, excite disturbances, lead to revelings and retard our advancement in intelligence, respectability, usefulness and piety." He also said that, as was the case with slaveholding, it was not merely the abuse of the practice but the practice itself that needed abolition.[59]

Another area that black people wanted to participate in was the military. Black people in Rhode Island had distinguished themselves in the Revolution and in the War of 1812, but as the nineteenth century progressed, the new nation made it clear that it wanted only white men to bear arms. In peacetime, the federal government no longer needed the black population that had been an asset in the Revolution and in 1792 passed legislation restricting the militia to white men.[60] In response, black communities throughout the North sponsored private militia companies. Other groups sponsored similar organizations because many in early nineteenth-century America were martially inclined. Private companies allowed the camaraderie of the drill without the discipline found in state-run units. Whites were able to choose between private and state-sponsored military companies; blacks could join only those private organizations that they formed.[61]

The African Greys, the black military company of Providence, first appeared at the opening of the African Union Meeting House in 1821. A self-dubbed colonel, George Barrett, a War of 1812 veteran, acted as the group's commander. At the opening of the African Union Meeting House, the African Greys marched as an escort unit for the church. The young men who joined the company provided their own muskets. Moses Brown, the Quaker patron of the African Union Meeting House, objected to the carrying of muskets and convinced the company to leave their arms outside the church.[62]

The African Greys, the black military company of Providence, ing in regional military parades where other private militia companies went. One such parade was held in Providence. Military companies from all over the Northeast came, including an Irish company from Philadelphia.[63] However ceremonial the company might have been, it served a more pressing need. The fear of attack and the feeling that the law would not assist them made many blacks feel that training in the use of arms was one way to provide self-protection. This belief would bear fruit later in the 1840s when a private black military company helped to put down the Dorr rebellion, the effort of working-class whites to get the vote. Because of this action, anti-Dorr forces in Rhode Island restored black voting rights in 1842.[64]

Two processes led to the development of black institutions in Providence. Physical independence caused black people in Providence to seek solutions to the problems that confronted them. Growing racism dictated that these solutions would be in separate institutions. The story does not end here, for the black people of Providence found that these black institutions were only a temporary solution. Black schools could educate children, black churches minister to the religious needs of black worshippers, black societies confer status on their members, but more would be needed. The rights that others had were desired by Providence's free Negroes. To receive these rights and the protections and benefits that society could bestow meant political activism, work for legal equality. That would be the next step.

Notes

1. Alice Felt Tyler, *Freedom's Ferment* (New York: Harper, 1962), pp. 1-21; Carl Russell Fish, *The Rise of the Common Man* (New York: Macmillan, 1927).

2. James Truslow Adams, "Disenfranchisement of Negroes in New England," *American Historical Review* 30 (April 1925): 543-47; Leon F. Litwack, *North of Slavery* (Chicago: University of Chicago Press, 1961), p. 32.

3. Fox, "The Negro Vote in Old New York," pp. 96-97; Adams, "Disenfranchisement of Negroes, pp. 543-47. Adams noted that black voters in Boston had a similar swing effect. See also E. S. Abdy, *Journal of a Residence and Tour in the United States II* (London, 1835), p. 8; Litwack, *North of Slavery*, pp. 75-81.

4. Fox, "Negro Vote," pp. 97-98.

5. Adams, "Disenfranchisement of Negroes," p. 545; Benjamin Franklin Wilbur, *Little Compton Families* (Little Compton, R.I.: Little Compton Historical Society, 1974), p. 520; William H. Robinson, *Blacks in 19th Century Rhode Island: An Overview* (Providence: Rhode Island Black Heritage Society, 1978), p. 66.

6. Arline Ruth Kiven, *Then Why the Negroes* (Providence: Urban League of Rhode Island, 1973), p. 8.

7. William H. Robinson, ed., *The Proceedings of the Free African Union Society and the African Benevolent Society: Newport, Rhode Island 1780-1824* (Providence: Urban League of Rhode Island, 1976).

8. Ibid., letter no. 15, p. 26.

9. Ibid., letter no. 38, "Brethren of the Union Society in Newport," p. 43.

10. Ibid., pp. 152-196.

11. Ibid., p. 19.

12. Ibid., p. 146.

13. George Arnold Salvador, *Paul Cuffee, The Black Yankee* (New Bedford, Mass.: Reynolds-DeWalt Printing, 1969), p. 24.

14. U.S. Census, 1790 (manuscript).

15. It is significant that the African elections continued into the 1830s, with white employers continuing to sponsor black candidates.

16. Brown, *The Life of William J. Brown*, pp. 40-41.

17. Ibid., p. 46.

18. Ibid., p. 41.

19. Ibid., p. 49.

20. Ibid., p. 58.

21. Ibid.

22. U.S. Census, 1820 (manuscript).

23. Brown, *Life of Brown*, p. 33.

24. Ibid., pp. 32-33.

25. Ibid., pp. 126-27.

26. *Providence Gazette*, October 23, 1824.

27. Brown, *Life of Brown*, p. 89.

28. Ibid.

29. *Hardscrabble Calendar: Report of the Trials of Oliver Cummins, Nathaniel G. Metcalf, Gilbert Hines and Arthur Farrier* (Providence, 1824), introduction.

30. Ibid., pp. 5-21.

31. Ibid.

32. Ibid., pp. 15-16. Italics added.

33. Brown, *Life of Brown*, pp. 89-90.

34. Ibid., p. 93.

35. Ibid., pp. 94-95; *Providence Journal*, September 26, 1831.

36. Irving Bartlett, *From Slave to Citizen; The Story of the Negro in Rhode Island* (Providence: Urban League of Greater Providence, 1954), pp. 32-33; *Providence Journal*, September 24, 1831.

37. Brown, *Life of Brown*, p. 96; Bartlett, *From Slave to Citizen*, pp. 33-34.

38. Rammelkamp, "The Providence Negro Community, 1820-1842," p. 91; Kiven, *Then Why the Negroes*, p. 46.

39. Brown, *Life of Brown*, p. 46. The British traveler J. S. Buckingham observed that some blacks continued to attend white churches in

Providence after the founding of black churches. In 1841 he observed that blacks were still in segregated sections of white churches in Providence. J. S. Buckingham, *America, Historical, Statistic and Descriptive,* vol. 3 (London, 1841), p. 491.

40. *A Short History of the African Union Meeting House* (Providence, 1821), p. 23.

41. Ibid., p. 13.

42. Ibid., p. 4.

43. U.S. Census, 1820 (manuscript).

44. *Short History of the African Union Meeting House,* p. 5.

45. Brown, *Life of Brown,* p. 49; *Short History of the African Union Meeting House,* p. 9.

46. *Short History of the African Union Meeting House,* p. 6.

47. Ibid.

48. Ibid., p. 4.

49. Ibid., pp. 12, 30.

50. Ibid., p. 29; Diane Ravitch, *The Great School Wars* (New York: Basic Books, 1974), pp. 12-16.

51. Brown, *Life of Brown,* pp. 48-49.

52. Ibid., p. 88.

53. Thomas B. Stockwell, *A History of Public Education in Rhode Island* (Providence: Providence Press Co., 1876), pp. 51, 169, 189.

54. Rammelkamp, "Providence Negro Community," p. 90.

55. Ibid.

56. Ibid.

57. *Minutes of a Convention of People of Color for the Promotion of Temperance in New England* (Providence: H. H. Brown, 1836).

58. Ibid., p. 10.

59. Ibid., pp. 12-13.

60. Litwack, *North of Slavery,* p. 32.

61. Oscar Handlin, *Boston Immigrants* (Cambridge: Harvard University Press, 1959), p. 157. Handlin notes that Irish immigrants formed militia companies that "were primarily social organizations less attractive for their martial exploits than for the small bounty, the opportunity to parade in uniform and the dinner and speeches that followed target practice and parade."

62. Brown, *Life of Brown,* pp. 83-84.

63. Ibid., p. 56.

64. Ibid., p. 174; Rammelkamp, "Providence Negro Community," p. 93

POLITICAL
ACTIVITY

3

During the 1830s, the frustrations of Providence's black inhabitants grew even as their wealth, education, and church attendance increased. By 1840 Providence blacks had come far in their efforts to participate in the social order that was emerging in ante-bellum America. The African Union Meeting House had become the Meeting Street Baptist Church. Three other black churches, the Second Freewill Baptist Church, the Zion Methodist Church, and Christ Church (Episcopal), were also formed to minister to the needs of black worshippers. The privately and publicly supported schools were responsible for a 50 percent literacy rate among Providence's black population by 1840. According to one estimate, roughly 10 percent of the black population was attending school by 1839.[1]

There were impressive accomplishments for a population that had been excluded from participation in the larger society's institutions and had just established its first institutions barely a generation before. These accomplishments also heightened awareness of the discrimination and consequent deprivations that Providence blacks were made to endure. From the ranks of Providence's black community came those who questioned why education, profession of religion, and property holding did not suffice to make one equal, permit one to vote or send one's child to the common schools. The first generation of independent black leadership in Providence, those who had established independent households in the 1810s and 1820s, had started off with the formation of the African Union Meeting House. These first leaders could do little more than establish parallel institutions, hoping that church, school, lodge, militia company, and temperance society activities could furnish evidence of the worth ness of the black community. Their successors in the 1830s and 1840s could, with these accomplishments as a foundation, demand more.

These new demands were to be aimed at the caste system that mandated a separate and inferior role for black Rhode Islanders. In virtually every phase of life—the state law restricting voting to whites, separate schooling, prohibitions on blacks working in taverns, discrimination on steamships—Rhode Island made the subordination of blacks ever present. The first target of the black reformers was the white-only suffrage restriction. Rhode Island blacks, largely because of the efforts of Providence activists, managed to regain the suffrage. This was the only case in antebellum America where blacks who had been disenfranchised managed to regain the vote.[2]

This reenfranchisement and the subsequent political behavior of blacks exacerbated the tensions that had developed between blacks and lower- and working-class whites. It also increased black dependence on and orientation toward the more aristocratic elements of the white community. The patron-client links that originated in slavery and that were renewed during the formation of the African Union Meeting House were strengthened and expanded with the development of black political activity. An insight into black political activity can be gained by examining black efforts to regain suffrage, especially during the Dorr rebellion, and by examining subsequent black political behavior during the election of 1848 and during the attempt to integrate schools in the 1850s.

Suffrage and the Dorr War

Rhode Island was a conservative state. The leveling and egalitarian impulses of Jacksonian democracy had not fully extended to that state. While other states dropped property as a requisite

for suffrage, Rhode Island held firm; the workingman was not
to be permitted to participate in affairs of state unless he owned
a $134 freehold. One impulse of the Jacksonian era did reach
Rhode Island; in 1822 the state restricted the vote to white men.
The 1830s thus became a time when poor whites and blacks attempted to secure the vote.[3]

In the late 1830s, town officials in Providence took notice
of the growing property ownership by Negroes and decided to
levy taxes on black-held property. Those blacks who were affected met in the African Union Meeting House to discuss the
issue of taxation in the absence of representation. Laborer
George C. Willis and barber Alfred Niger became chairman and
secretary, respectively, of a committee to plead the cause of
black suffrage. The committee, which included George McCarthy,
a trader, Edward Barnes, a farmer, Ichabod Northup, a small
businessman, and James Harris, went to the Rhode Island General
Assembly. William Brown reported:

After the feeling was understood by those who had spoken, they appointed
a committee to meet the next general assembly, and inform them of their
disapproval to meet the tax, for they were unwilling to be taxed and not
allowed to be represented. Some of the members of the house said it was
perfectly right; if the colored people were to be taxed they should be
represented. But the members of the house from Newport were bitterly
opposed to colored people being represented, saying: "Shall a Nigger be
allowed to go to the polls and tie my vote? No, Mr. Speaker, it can't be.
The taxes don't amount to more than forty or fifty dollars; let them be
taken off."[4]

At the same time, white workingmen began questioning their
exclusion from the polls. In 1833 a group of white workingmen
from backgrounds very similar to those of the black suffrage advocates began agitating for the abolition of the property qualification. This group, headed by William J. Tillinghast, a barber,
Lawrence Richards, a blacksmith, William Mitchell, a shoemaker,
Seth Luther, a house carpenter, William Miller, a currier, and
David Brown, a clock maker, held weekly meetings in the Providence town hall. In May 1833 the group published an address
that argued the cause of free suffrage. This group pressed for a

suffrage contingent on meeting responsibilities to the state that the poor would not find impossible. They argued that Rhode Island should model itself after Massachusetts, permitting the vote to those who either served in the militia or paid taxes.[5]

This document, *An Address on the Right of Free Suffrage*, attacked Rhode Island's property qualification as a feudal remnant. Throughout the address, republicanism and democracy were upheld, feudalism and inherited privilege disparaged. Seth Luther likened the condition of Rhode Island's nonfreeholders to that of slaves. The concept of the equality of man was espoused in this document, while race was not mentioned; and the reaffirmation of the Declaration of Independence's statement of man's equality augured for some receptivity to the idea of black suffrage. Still, blacks were not part of this suffrage movement.[6]

While blacks and poor whites pled their separate cases for enfranchisement, Thomas Wilson Dorr was becoming a rebel. A catholic Jacksonian, Dorr combined the democratic-egalitarian impulses of the early nineteenth century and an advocacy of racial equality with his Whig-aristocratic background. From a prosperous family, Dorr attended Phillips Exeter Academy and Harvard College; later he read law and embarked upon a political career. As a Rhode Island state legislator, he was active in public school reform, the abolition movement (he helped to kill a proposal that would have banned abolitionist activity in Rhode Island), and the suffrage extension movement.[7]

The 1830s was a frustrating decade for suffrage extension advocates. By 1837, Dorr had renounced his Whig affiliations because of that party's resistance to suffrage extension. The dispute over suffrage made Dorr a Democrat; by 1839, he was an unsuccessful Democratic candidate for Congress. Though a Democrat, Dorr retained his abolitionist sympathies.[8]

The election of 1840 was a watershed in the history of the Rhode Island suffrage movement. In the spring of 1840, the Rhode Island Suffrage Association brought together working class whites who had been active in the suffrage extension movements of the 1830s. A constitution was written that, among other things, specified that the association wanted to extend suffrage to all native-born white males. As 1840 moved on, intensive political campaigning politicized many, increasing interest in the suffrage extension movement and the Rhode Island Suffrage Association. One commentator unsympathetic to the association or Suffrage party noted that the election of 1840 dashed the hope of many Suffrage Association advocates, causing an increase in their political activity.[9]

The activities of the Suffrage Association held out renewed hope for the advocates of black suffrage. If the property qualification was to be questioned, why should the racial barrier be allowed to stand? The association's statements were ambiguous enough to cause black activists to believe that it would be sympathetic to joining forces with proponents of black suffrage. The Suffrage Association continued to put forth Massachusetts's voting requirements as the ideal that Rhode Island should adopt. Providence blacks were well aware that their Massachusetts counterparts had the right to vote. The other state that the Rhode Island Suffrage Association held out as a model was New York, which permitted universal white manhood suffrage and limited black manhood suffrage. Suffrage Association statements constantly compared the position of workingmen in Rhode Island with that of southern slaves; these statements indicated disapproval of the conditions of both groups. Abolitionists' sentiments were sometimes expressed in the Suffrage Association's newspaper, *The New Age and Constitutional Advocate*. And, of course, Thomas Dorr had been a champion of abolitionist activity.[10]

Despite the fact that the 1840 constitution of the Suffrage Association specified that the organization was seeking universal suffrage for white men, throughout early 1841 blacks and abolitionists participated in Suffrage Association activities, encouraged by signs that a possibility for making common cause existed. Black men voted in Suffrage Association elections. The Suffrage Association, having decided that mass organization, people's conventions, and association elections would popularize their cause, allowed wide participation, including black participation in their activities.[11]

By late summer and early fall 1841, the confrontation over whether the Suffrage Association would be a universal suffrage movement or a white-only movement was coming to a head. In early September the issue began to heat up when one Suffrage Association assembly in Providence excluded black participants. One association partisan, writing in the *Providence Journal*, tells of the political tightrope the association was walking, attempting to alienate neither abolitionist sentiment nor the more general prejudices of the day:

Much fault has been found with the Association by some cavaliers, because upon their own principles they do not seem inclined to admit our colored brethren to an equal participation in suffrage. It is said, if "all men are born free and equal," if, "the right to vote be a natural and inalienable right," . . . why does the mere accident of color make a difference?

A scene occurred on Christian Hill, in this city growing out of the exclusion of a respectable colored man from voting at the election of delegates to the People's Convention, which gave much cause for regret to some of the friends of free suffrage, and which, it seems to us, might easily have been avoided by a little more caution in the wording of the call on the part of the association. The call certainly included our colored friends, and in some wards of the city a few of the lighter colored were allowed, there being no objection, to vote. But we know that, as a general rule, the Association thought it might be too great a shock to public sentiment to allow colored men the privilege, although as a matter of consistency, and to avoid giving offense to our abolitionist friends, the call was so worded as to include them.[12]

The Suffrage Association partisan, who signed his letter "Town Born," went on to counsel blacks to be patient and support the Suffrage Association despite the fact that the organization was not taking up the cause of black suffrage. He stated that after the cause of universal white manhood suffrage had triumphed the Suffrage Association would help blacks attain the vote.[13]

Two days later, on September 17, the *Providence Journal* ran a letter from a black man responding to "Town Born." It said in part:

From some of the views expressed by "Town Born," in his last number, I am compelled to dissent. If I do not misunderstand him, he is disposed in accommodation to the unreasonable prejudices of the country, to exclude, even under the new dispensation, the approach of which he hails with so much delight, our colored fellow citizens from the right to vote and to be elected to office. To be sure, he encourages them with the prospect of redress, at a different day, when the full blessings of universal suffrage shall come to be felt throughout our borders. In this matter however, I would submit to no delay, consent to no compromise.[14]

Later in September, the issue of black participation in the association heated up when Alfred Niger, one of the leaders of the unsuccessful black suffrage movement a few years earlier, attended a Suffrage Association meeting. During the meeting held September 24, 1841, Niger was nominated by a majority of the executive committee for the position of association treasurer. A minority report had nominated Thomas Greene, a white member of the association, for the position. Members objected to the nomination of a black man for an important association position. The chairman wanted to set aside Niger's nomination, but members of the executive committee prevailed upon the chairman to hold the vote in order to determine which of the members had secret abolitionist leanings. The vote took place, and Greene was elected by an undisclosed margin.[15]

At the October convention of the Suffrage Association, a black delegation under the leadership of the Reverend Alexander Crummell appeared. Crummell, who had been active in the efforts of New York blacks to eliminate the property requirements for black voters, was pastor of Christ Church in Providence. Crummell and his delegation were introduced at the Suffrage Association convention by Thomas Dorr. A statement on behalf of Providence's black residents, written by Crummell and signed by men who had been in the Providence community for a longer period of time, was read before the convention:

GENTLEMEN: The remonstrance of the undersigned colored citizens of Rhode Island, respectfully represent, that, in the constitution that is proposed to be sent forth by your respected body for adoption, there is one measure inserted, upon which we, as an interested party, beg leave, with deference, to make known our views, and give an expression of our sentiments. We have reference to that proposed article which, in inserting the word "white," denies all persons of color the use and exercise of the elective franchise. . . .

Is a justification of our disfranchisement sought in our want of christian character? We point to our churches as our reputation. In our want of intelligence? We refer not merely to the schools supported by the State, for our advantage; but to the private schools, well filled and sustained, and taught by competent teachers of our own people. Is our industry questioned? This day, were there no complexional hindrance, we could present a more than proportionate number of our people, who might immediately, according to the freeholders' qualification, become voters.[16]

The convention debated whether to adopt black suffrage as one of its goals. Dorr called the exclusion of blacks unjust. Another speaker prophetically warned his fellow delegates that by their failure to include blacks, "we plant a dagger in the bosom of our cause." Others argued that including blacks in the movement would increase the movement's difficulties, make the Suffrage Association unpopular, and ensure the cause's defeat. By a vote of forty-six to eighteen, the convention decided to retain its white-only constitution.[17] In October the Suffrage Association adopted a constitution that in part read:

Every white male citizen of the United States, of the age of twenty-one years, who had resided in this state for one year, and in any town, city, or district of the same for six months next preceding the election at which he offers to vote, shall be an elector of all officers who are elected, or may hereafter be made eligible by the people.[18]

The hostilities many lower- and working-class whites felt toward blacks, coupled with the fear of linking their movement with the unpopular abolitionist effort, brought about the Suffrage Association's white-only posture. This placed Dorr and other supporters of the movement who had previously indicated problack sympathies, William Goodell and Frances McDougal, among others, in a delicate position. Their inclinations toward abolitionism and black betterment and their desire for a more democratic suffrage clashed. One way that many of these people managed to resolve this dilemma was to note that the freeholdholders, who had formed the Law and Order party, did not favor black suffrage. Another argument was that the "Peoples Constitution" contained a provision that submitted the white-only clause to public referendum. When put to popular referendum, the white-only clause was retained.[19]

While the Suffrage Association was excluding blacks from its movement, the freeholders were also reaffirming their belief in the undesirability of black voting. The Legal Convention, held in November 1841, fearing the pressure of the Suffrage Association, drafted a constitution that permitted native-born white men to vote without property qualification. Foreign-born whites would be required to meet the $134 freehold in order to qualify as voters, while blacks were to be denied voting rights altogether.[20]

At this point both sides met with the disfavor of Providence blacks and the public criticism of national antislavery figures. Frederick Douglass noted his disgust with both factions. The *Liberator* ran a letter decrying the use of the term *Peoples Constitution* to describe the Suffrage Association's constitution, noting that it referred only to the white portion of the population. Tension grew between the Suffrage Association and blacks and abolitionists as the latter denounced the Peoples Constitution for its exclusion. Suffrage Association people in turn attacked blacks and abolitionists as tools of the landholders who sought to discredit the suffrage movement. Abolitionist speakers, who had never gotten a very friendly reception in Providence, were attacked by Suffrage Association members. In January 1842, abolitionist speaker Abby Kelly was pelted with snowballs by a Suffrage party mob as she attempted to speak in Providence.[21]

By 1842 the Suffrage party was in open rebellion, having declared Thomas Dorr to be governor of the state. The landholders, or Law and Order party, fearing the Suffrage party and the possibility that it might bring about a government dominated by white workingmen, particularly Irish immigrants, softened their attitudes toward the black community. With the competing governments that Rhode Island had by May 1842, the Rhode Island establishment was apprehensive.[22]

That apprehension increased as the Suffrage party decided to march on Providence. This solidified the growing relationship between the landholders and the black community. Where black exclusion by the Suffrage party had previously been only a landholder's propaganda point, it became a very concrete way of maintaining power.

As was the case during the crisis of the Revolution and the War of 1812 and as would later occur during the Civil War, necessity overcame prejudice; blacks would bear arms to defend

the Rhode Island government. Black men, some previously associated with the African Greys, were organized into home
guard units in Providence.[23]

Some two hundred black men met in Providence to form a
home guard company. It was an opportunity for status and
recognition that had previously been denied Providence blacks.
Instead of the mock ceremony of the African Greys, they were
to receive genuine recognition from the state in this time of
crisis. They began to elect officers. Three black men campaigned
to officer the two black companies that had been formed. The
three reflected the different criteria that the black community
used in selecting its leadership. One of the candidates was
Thomas Howland, a stevedore with little education who nonetheless had been able to amass a fair amount of property. Another, James Hazzard, described by Brown as "the richest
colored man in the city," was a clothing dealer who "thought
the command belonged to him."[24] The third candidate was a
poor but well-read barber named Peterson. He sought the command, but his candidacy was the weakest. While the campaigning for office was going on, Peterson cautioned against enthusiasm in this military endeavor. Like many other educated black
of the period, Peterson was familiar with the black role in the
Revolution and the War of 1812. He told the audience of black
volunteers that during the Battle of New Orleans, Andrew Jackson had promised much to the free mulatto soldiers who helped
stem the British tide, but that after the battle, their services
were not rewarded. At that point the group decided that black
interests would be better served by enlisting in general home
guard units rather than forming the two black companies.[25]

The two hundred volunteers joined existing companies. Acting as part of the Providence home guard, they guarded vital
points in Providence and were conspicuous in protecting the
town against the threat of fire. The arming of the black community by the state of Rhode Island had symbolic and concrete significance, part of the latter being blacks' ability to
protect themselves against Dorrite attacks, which had been
occurring in 1841 and 1842. One result of black activity against
what has been termed the Dorr rebellion was that the state of
Rhode Island continued to support a black militia unit after
the rebellion ceased.[26]

Another result was that the Law and Order party reexamined its position on black suffrage. The rebellion was crushed, Dorr had fled, and the Law and Order party held a convention in September 1842 to determine voting requirements. The events of the past year had convinced them of the need to permit universal suffrage for native-born white men. A suggestion was made at that convention that a system somewhat similar to New York's practice should be adopted regarding black voting. This measure would have required blacks to have had a freehold before being permitted to vote. That motion was tabled. The convention decided instead to allow native-born males, both white and black, to vote on the same basis. Another motion requiring the foreign born to have a freehold passed. The Law and Order party simultaneously picked up an ally and made it difficult for their antagonists, the Irish, to vote.[27]

The Dorr rebellion placed Rhode Island blacks in a unique position. While other states had disenfranchised blacks, none restored black voting rights before the Civil War. Even New York, where blacks, needed a $250 freehold in order to vote, did not equalize requirements for black and white electors until after the Civil War, though black voters were Whig stalwarts in several elections. Blacks had been reenfranchised in Rhode Island, and the Law and Order party had use for their new-found allies.[28]

The Negro-Whig Alliance

Black and abolitionist political activity was not particularly welcome in Providence. Nonetheless, the Law and Order party recognized that the newly enfranchised black voter would be a valuable ally, faithful to those who had enfranchised him, fearful of those who blocked this recognition of his equality. The party thus developed a machine that operated in the Providence black community. It returned little on the investment of black loyalty that it received, yet it continued to receive loyalty from the black community because there existed no other viable options.[29]

Nominally changed from opponents to proponents of black political equality by the Dorr rebellion, the Law and Order party let its support of the political equality of black and white remain largely symbolic. A Whig[30] commentator recalling the events of the Dorr rebellion stressed the white-only clause in the Suffrage party's constitution, neglecting to mention that the freeholders only reluctantly became champions of black suffrage.[31]

Outside of these reminders, the Law and Order party did little for blacks. The Law and Order governor of Rhode Island proclaimed his opposition to jury trials for those alleged to be fugitive slaves in 1843, and in Providence Whig politicians drove a politically active (and presumably too independent) black man out of town. A year later, the Rhode Island Ladies Anti-Slavery Society had difficulty renting a room in Providence even though nonpolitical black social organizations managed to find meeting places. Southern masters were permitted to bring their slaves to Rhode Island so they could enjoy their summer resorts in Newport. Schools remained segregated.[32]

Still, the cementing of the Whig-Negro alliance continued. The enfranchisement of black men in Rhode Island added between seven hundred and a thousand potential voters to the state's electorate during the 1840s. This was a significant number, a number that Whig forces in the state could not ignore. Although the black population barely exceeded 2 percent of the total population of the state in the years between 1842 and 1860, black men were often a much higher percentage of the potential and actual electorate. In several statewide elections where voter turnout was low, black voters could have accounted for nearly 10 percent of the votes cast. In one statewide election, the gubernatorial race of 1845, the Law and Order party lost the contest by a little over two hundred votes. The next year, 1846, the party regained the governship by a slim margin of fewer than one hundred votes. (See table 3-1.) In both elections, the state's highest office was determined by a margin far smaller than the size of the potential black electorate of the state, indeed far smaller than the three hundred to four hundred actual voters that William Brown, who was paid by the Law and Order party to bring out the black vote, indicated actually voted in Providence.[33]

The small size of the Rhode Island electorate contributed to the importance of the black vote. None of the antebellum elections brought more than 24,000 voters to the polls, a number brought fewer than 10,000; most of the contests attracted between 10,000 and 20,000 electors. (See tables 3-1 and 3-2.) This meant that in even the most popular contests, blacks could account for as much as 4 to 6 percent of the electorate. In one election, the gubernatorial race of 1850, only about 4,500 men cast their votes (table 3-2); blacks potentially could have been over 20 percent of the electorate in that race. One reason that the size of the electorate was so small was that the property qualification screened out large numbers of the foreign born. Although the foreign-born population was nearly ten times the size of the black population, the size of the black electorate was at least equal to and probably greater than the size of the foreign-born electorate in the antebellum period.[34]

In Providence the black vote played a significant role in local politics. Evidence indicates that contests were close. Providence was an industrial town with white workingmen who voted for the Democratic and other parties that opposed the Law and Order party. Whig forces in Providence, including the virulently anti-Democrat and anti-Irish *Providence Journal*, looked to the black voter to provide the margin of victory in close contests. Two illustrations of how close elections in Providence could be and how critical the black vote could be in determining Whig success or failure are provided by the gubernatorial races of 1843 and 1845. In the 1843 election, Law and Order candidate James Fenner carried the city of Providence by 150 votes, defeating his Democratic opponent Thomas F. Carpenter by 2,632 to 2,482 votes. Without the 300 to 400 black voters of Providence, Fenner would not have carried the city. In 1845 Fenner lost the vote in Providence by a margin of 113 votes to Liberation party candidate Charles Jackson. Jackson received 2,625 votes in Providence and Fenner received 2,512, a margin narrow enough to be accounted for by a simple falling off of the number of black voters. The implications of these narrow margins in statewide elections that brought out large numbers of voters (table 3-1) for local contests are clear. The returns for the presidential election of 1844 also confirm that blacks played a critical role in Providence's elections. In that year, the Whig candidate, Henry Clay, received 3,751 votes in Providence Coun-

Table 3-1
POTENTIAL IMPACT OF THE BLACK VOTE IN ANTEBELLUM RHODE ISLAND:
SELECTED STATEWIDE ELECTIONS IN THE 1840s

YEAR AND TYPE	CANDIDATE	PARTY	VOTE TOTALS	ESTIMATE OF ELIGIBLE BLACK VOTERS[a]	BLACKS AS POTENTIAL PERCENTAGE OF ELECTORS[b]
1843 (gubernatorial)	James Fenner	Law and Order	9,140		
	Thomas F. Carpenter	Democratic	7,393		
			16,533 (all parties)	700	4
1844 (presidential)	Henry Clay	Whig	7,322		
	James K. Polk	Democratic	4,867		
			12,189 (all parties)	700	6
1845 (gubernatorial)	James Fenner	Law and Order	7,699		
	Charles Jackson	Liberation	7,900		
			15,599 (all parties)	700	6
1846 (gubernatorial)	Byron Diman	Law and Order	7,477		
	Charles Jackson	Liberation	7,391		
	Others		155		
			15,023 (all parties)	1,000	7
1847 (gubernatorial)	Elisha Harris	Whig	6,300		
	Olney Ballou	Democratic	4,350		
			743		

80

1848 (presidential)	Zachary Taylor	Whig	6,705		
	Lewis Cass	Democratic	3,613		
	Martin Van Buren	Free Soil	726		
			11,393 (all parties)	1,000	9
1849 (gubernatorial)	Henry Anthony	Whig	5,081		
	Adnah Sackett	Democratic	2,964		
	Edward Harris	Free Soil	458		
	Others		112		
			8,615 (all parties)	1,000	12

SOURCE: Interuniversity Consortium on Political and Social Research, University of Michigan.

a These figures, taken from the U.S. censuses of 1840 and 1850, measure only potential impact of the black vote. They do not constitute a claim that all eligible black voters actually voted in every election or that they voted at a disproportionately higher rate than the rest of the electorate.

b Rounded to the nearest whole number. Calculated by dividing the estimate of eligible black voters by the vote totals for all parties.

Table 3-2
POTENTIAL IMPACT OF THE BLACK VOTE IN ANTEBELLUM RHODE ISLAND:
SELECTED STATEWIDE ELECTIONS IN THE 1850s

YEAR AND TYPE	CANDIDATE	PARTY	VOTE TOTALS	ESTIMATE OF ELIGIBLE BLACK VOTERS[a]	BLACKS AS POTENTIAL PERCENTAGE OF ELECTORS[b]
1850 (gubernatorial)	Henry B. Anthony	Whig	3,629		
	Edward Harris	Free Soil	761		
	Others		133		
			4,523 (all parties)	1,000	22
1851 (gubernatorial)	Philip Allen	Democratic	6,958		
	Josiah Chapin	Whig	6,071		
	Edward Harris	Free Soil	184		
	Others		18		
			13,231 (all parties)	1,000	8
1852 (presidential)	Winfield Scott	Whig	7,626		
	Franklin Pierce	Democratic	8,735		
	John P. Hale	Free Soil	644		
			17,005 (all parties)	1,000	6
1854 (gubernatorial)	William P. Hoppin	Whig	9,112		
	Francis M. Diamond	Democratic	6,484		
			15,596 (all parties)	1,000	6

		Democrat	6,680	
	John C. Fremont	Republican	11,467	
	Millard Fillmore	American (Know-Nothing)	1,675	
			19,822 (all parties)	1,000	5
1860 (gubernatorial)	Seth Padelford	Republican	10,835	
	William Sprague	Union	12,295	
			143	
			23,273 (all parties)	1,000	4
1860 (presidential)	Stephen A. Douglas	Northern Democrat	7,707	
	Abraham Lincoln	Republican	12,244	
			19,951 (all parties)	1,000	5

SOURCE: Interuniversity Consortium on Political and Social Research.

a From U.S. censuses of 1850 and 1860.
b Rounded to the nearest whole number.

ty; his opponent, Democratic candidate James Polk, received 3,192 votes. Clay's margin in the county was 559 votes. Between 54 percent and 72 percent, depending on whether one accepts Brown's lower or higher estimate, of Clay's margin could be attributed to blacks in the city of Providence. If one adds blacks in the rest of the county who would have been eligible to vote in that election, probably there were around 467 black voters in all of Providence County, and they would have accounted for approximately 84 percent of Clay's margin of victory.[35]

Recognizing that the black vote could determine the outcome in elections, the Law and Order party wanted this group of electors to come to the polls. In the early 1840s a number of black voters who were illiterate stopped voting. They were embarrassed because Whig officials would write their votes for them, giving public evidence of their lack of education.

The Law and Order party reacted quickly to make sure that this decline among black voters did not threaten its dominance. Blacks who failed to vote were threatened with the loss of their jobs if they worked for Whig employers. Those beholden to Whig charity were threatened with the cutoff of such largesse if they did not show up at the polls.[36]

Because of this crisis of diminishing black votes, the Whigs also began turning to indigenous black leadership in an effort to maintain high levels of black voting. Black voters were given private assistance to help them prepare their ballots. The Young Men's Union Friend Society, a group that had originated in the African Union Meeting House, was enlisted to help get out the black vote. William J. Brown became, in effect, a ward healer, paid by the Law and Order party to ensure that black men came to the polls. A room was rented before election time to help black voters sign their names to envelopes bearing the ballot. Brown ensured that they voted the Law and Order ticket.[37]

In addition to coercion and the employment of black community leaders, the Law and Order party threw parties for black voters at election time to ensure their voting. Just before an election, black leaders and Law and Order party officials would gather black voters and feed them coffee, crackers, cheese, and shaved beef. Special effort was made to bring lower-class black voters to these events before the Democrats could get them.[38]

Thus fortified, the voters would be moved en masse to the polls where they would deposit their ballots. In many ways the Law and Order preelection festivities were similar to the kinds of celebrations that had preceded the African Governors' elections in the eighteenth century. This time the festivities would be put to the service of nineteenth-century partisan politics. In many ways, the techniques used to secure the votes of blacks were similar to the methods used to mobilize the votes of other ethnic groups in different political machines.[39]

While the Law and Order party developed its procedures for mobilizing the black electorate, Democratic behavior reinforced black voting patterns. Black voters were threatened by Democratic partisans. Democrats declared that blacks sold their votes for crackers and cheese. At the preelection parties held by the Whigs for black voters, black men brought muskets to ensure that their voting efforts would not be interrupted by Democrats.

Despite their fidelity, blacks continued to derive only two benefits from their association with the Law and Order party. One was the courting of the black vote that occurred during election times. This courting with its attendant paying of ward healers and supplying of cheer to the rank and file was, of course, a temporary, election-time phenomenon. The other benefit blacks derived was the continuation of a state-supported militia company. State support of this company was unique. Even Massachusetts, which had recognized black statute equality since the late eighteenth century, felt that federal law prohibited it from having a black militia unit supported with state funds. This benefit that blacks derived was also clearly related to the threat of Suffrage party resurgence.[40]

The Election of 1848

The election of 1848 put the black-Whig alliance to its most severe test when it created an ideological and political dilemma for the black voters of Providence and sparked intense interest on the part of national black and antislavery figures in black Providence's political proclivities as well. Interest and ideology, national black leadership, and local patron-client links all clashed as black voters in Providence worked to sort out a dilemma.[41]

Rhode Island voters in 1848 had a three-way choice for the presidential election. Zachary Taylor, the Whig candidate, was a southern slaveholder. Lewis Cass, the Democrat, was an advocate of popular sovereignty. Dissident Democrats had formed the Free-Soil party, which was opposed to the expansion of slavery in the territories recently acquired in the Mexican War. Their candidate was New York Democrat and former president Martin Van Buren. Conscience Whigs, Free-Soil Democrats, and abolitionists combined to run Van Buren, and Charles Francis Adams, son of antislavery president John Quincy Adams, for president and vice-president, respectively. This ticket ran in Rhode Island and other northern states. Its "Free-Soil, Free Speech, Free Labor and Free Men" slogan met with approval by black and antislavery leaders throughout the Northeast.[42]

Cass, the Democratic candidate, seems never to have been considered seriously by the black voters of Providence. The dilemma was whether to vote for Taylor, the southern slaveholder but also the Whig, the candidate of black voters' political benefactors, or for Martin Van Buren, former Democrat. As a Democrat Van Buren had been no stalwart of black causes. He had previously opposed black settlement in western lands, supported continued slavery in the District of Columbia, and was opposed to eliminating the special property qualification for black voters in New York State.[43] By 1848, however, his position on these issues had softened somewhat, prompting Frederick Douglass's observation:

This was penned before Mr. Van Buren's letter accepting his nomination was published which affords some excuse of his palpable unfairness. Mr. Van Buren has declared his willingness to sign a bill for the abolition of slavery in the District of Columbia. We think the party should have been judged of in the light of its platform. So judged, friend Ward would never have supposed that voting for Van Buren could possibly be voting for slavery in the District of Columbia. . . . The course of the colored voters should not be determined by the past transgressions of the members of the "Free Soil" party, but by what they now are, and what they are now aiming to accomplish.[44]

There was a concerted effort in the black and antislavery presses during the summer of 1848 to convince blacks not to vote for Zachary Taylor. Directed primarily to New York's black voters, these articles reached black voters in Providence. The *North Star* recorded the appeals of New York black leader S. R. Ward and Frederick Douglass, both of whom advised against the client relation with the Whig party.[45]

The posture of black and abolitionist papers toward the black favoring of the Whig party reveals an interesting division between national figures on the one hand and local leaders and rank-and-file black voters on the other. In New York, where there was perhaps the longest tradition of black suffrage, despite the property qualification, black voters had an unbroken history of supporting first the Federalist and then the Whig parties. By 1848, black voters, whose numbers have been estimated as low as 1,000 and as high as 4,000, held the balance of power in some counties in New York State. According to one modern historian, 95 percent of this black vote went to Whig candidates.[46]

Antislavery leaders constantly pointed out how little blacks got in return for this loyalty to the Whig party. Lydia Maria Child in the *National Anti-Slavery Standard* pointed to intimidation of black voters in Providence by Whig officials. The *Liberator* delighted in relating incidents in Providence where Law and Order officials attacked blacks and abolitionists. Frederick Douglass in New York made a concerted effort to keep the New York black electorate, and one can assume black voters elsewhere, out of the Whig column in 1848.[47]

In Providence Free-Soil party members tried to convince blacks to vote with them and break their Whig ties. Those former Suffrage party people who had had abolitionist leanings joined the Free-Soil party, while those who had been in accord with the Suffrage party's antiblack posture stayed Democrats. Former fugitive slave Henry Bibb was brought up from New York to convince black voters to vote the Free-Soil ticket.[48]

The pro-Whig *Providence Journal* recognized the importance of the black vote in Providence and took steps to counter the pro-Van Buren campaign promulgated by black and other abolitionist leaders in the northeast. In late October the paper ran a sarcastic article, "The Reason Anti-Slavery Whigs Should Vote for Van Buren," telling of Van Buren's support for slavery in the District of Columbia, his willingness to surrender the Amistad captives into slavery, and his support of measures in Congress that would forbid debate on slavery.[49]

In early November 1848, the *Providence Journal* carried two articles specifically addressed to black voters and designed to ensure continued black loyalty to the Whig party. One article describing the situation from the Whig point of view predicted black fidelity to the Whig standard:

Very extraordinary efforts have been made by the Van Burenites to seduce the colored voters of this state to abandon the Whig party, which they have very greatly sustained, and to give their support to that branch of the Loco-foco party which is represented by Martin Van Buren who has done more to strengthen the institution of slavery than any other man north of Mason and Dixon's line.

The colored men of this city and state are a very respectable body of men. Orderly, industrious and intelligent and many of them possessed of a comfortable property. . . . The Whig party conferred upon the colored people the right of suffrage and elevated them to the rank of citizenship and the Whig party has a claim upon their gratitude which they have never failed to acknowledge at the polls.[50]

Two days later the *Providence Journal* addressed a specific appeal "To the Colored Voters":

The party which gave you the right to vote asks for your votes tomorrow. The men who have always stood by you ask you to stand by them. They ask you to do no new thing, to support no new principles, but only to stick by your old friends and your old principles. They ask you to stand by the Whig party, which is our party and your party;—the party of freedom and liberality and of all enlightened progress. . . .

You are asked to desert these men whom you knew to abandon this party that you have always acted with, and to vote for Martin Van Buren, a Locofoco, a Dorrite who has done more for slavery than any other Northern man. When Martin Van Buren was in office and could do something, he always acted against you and now that he is out of office and can do nothing, he talks for you. . . .

After having enjoyed the right of suffrage for six years and during all that time maintained the character of orderly citizens, will you now make Dorrites of yourselves by voting for Martin Van Buren. . . .

It is almost an insult to ask such questions. We know that you will not; we know that you will vote tomorrow just as you have always voted and will give another evidence of your attachment to correct principles and sound government.[51]

Displays of Free-Soil friendliness and the editorials of Douglass and Garrison did not prevail. Providence black voters supported the Whigs in 1848. At a meeting held by black voters prior to the election, George C. Willis, a leader in the early black suffrage struggle, spoke in favor of Zachary Taylor. While he acknowledged the evil of Taylor's slaveholding, he proclaimed the black interest in the Whig party. At this same meeting others denounced the Democratic party for its antiblack posture. The crowd called for William J. Brown's opinion. He tells us:

I arose, addressed the president, and told the audience we were called together to settle a very grave question, which as citizens, it was our duty to decide which of the two parties we were to support. We were not to decide upon the man, but the party. If we were to decide on the candidate, it would be not to cast a vote for Taylor, for he is a slaveholder; and this I presume is the feeling of every colored voter, but we are identified with the Whig party, shutting his eyes against the candidate; as he is nothing more than a servant for the party.[52]

Of the three hundred to four hundred black voters in Providence in 1848, all but a handful voted for Whig Zachary Taylor. In the 1848 election in Providence County, Taylor received 3,533 votes, Cass 2,510 votes, and Van Buren 398 votes. This time blacks in the city of Providence accounted for between 29 and 39 percent of the county margin of victory for the Whig candidate. If the Van Buren and the Cass votes are combined, blacks in Providence accounted for between 48 and 64 percent of the Whig margin of victory in the country. Fear that a vote for Van Buren would be wasted and would help Cass partly explains this vote. The well-developed network of Negro-Whig relationships, coupled with the traditional friction with the Democrats, caused the community to vote against its ideological inclination and with those with whom they had developed personal ties.[53]

Having won reenfranchisement only because of serious division in the white community, black men in Providence carefully guarded this right, a right that was precarious during most of the 1840s. Suffrage party adherents were still strong in the 1840s and had considerable influence in Democratic party organization. Voting strictly for Whig candidates was a way to ensure that the faction of the white community that had proven

itself in favor of at least nominal black equality stayed in power
Any deviation from this pattern might have given the Democrats the opportunity to regain power and settle old scores with
the black community.[54]

The School Integration Struggle

From the time of the founding of the African Union Meeting
House, Providence blacks had viewed education, along with
religion, as the principal means of increasing the acceptability
of the black community. The community supported a school
in the African Union Meeting House in the early 1820s. The
community's hope was that the schools would, in addition to
providing education for black children, improve moral development, promote temperance, and increase church membership
and profession of Christianity. In short, the schools were to
help produce the kind of ideal black citizen that those who
participated in the African Union Meeting House, the temperance society, the Young Men's Union Friend Society, and the
other fraternal, social, and political organizations hoped would
nullify the negative image of free Negroes as crime ridden, vice
prone, and otherwise unfit for equal citizenship.[55]

When it established common schools in the 1830s, Rhode
Island apportioned funds for black children up to the age of
ten. In Providence there was free public education for white
students through high school. School districts had the local
option of deciding whether they would have integrated or racial
ly separated schools. Rural areas with small numbers of black
inhabitants permitted black children to attend common schools
Providence, Newport, and Bristol, towns with substantial black
populations, established separate schools for black children.[56]

The Meeting Street and Pond Street schools were the two
black common schools in Providence supported by the state.
They supplanted the African Union Meeting House. In Providence in the 1850s schools were divided into four categories:
high schools, grammar schools, intermediate schools, and primary schools. The Pond Street School was a primary school.
The Meeting Street School comprised a primary school and a
grammar school. Primary and intermediate schools were housed

in two-story buildings, the lower story reserved for one level and the upper for the other. In all, white students had available to them sixteen combined primary-intermediate schools and three purely primary schools. Spread throughout the city, white pupils could attend schools in their own wards while black pupils from all parts of the city were confined to the Meeting Street and Pond Street schools. There were separate grammar schools, except for the Meeting Street facility, and there was one city-wide high school. White pupils were thus able to attend three distinct grades of postprimary schools, while black pupils had one postprimary school that had to serve the function of intermediate, grammar, and high school.[57]

According to the auditor's report to the Providence School Committee in 1854, three black teachers were employed by the Providence school system that year. One taught in the Meeting Street Grammar School and was paid $500 for the year; the other two were in the Meeting Street and Pond Street primary schools. Their combined salary was $425 for the year, presumably $212.50 for each of them. Teachers in white grammar schools received nearly twice what their colleague in the Meeting Street School received; their salary averaged $966.67 per year. Teachers in the white primary schools averaged $262.50, $50 more per year than those in the black schools. Assistant teachers at the white primary schools were paid at the rate of full teachers in the black primary schools. The two black schools did not have assistant teachers. Instead they were forced to rely on the old Lancasterian method found in the African Union Meeting House School.[58]

The Meeting House and Pond Street schools were sources of both pride and frustration for different elements of the Providence community. The schools did provide a basic education for the community's children. Both schools received favorable comments from black and white commentators, including many whites who hoped to forestall integrationist activity on the part of blacks by assuring them that black children were receiving a good education. Pleased with the favorable attention the two schools received and conscious of the educational progress made during the 1830s, 1840s, and 1850s, many blacks were cautious about educational change.

Others questioned the separation. The knowledge that there had been integrated schools in eighteenth-century Newport and Providence caused some to question the segregated school system of the mid-nineteenth century. In a letter to the *Liberator* published on October 18, 1839, William J. Brown noted that eighteenth-century schools were integrated in Newport and contrasted this with the then existing segregation. He also expressed the opinion that there were schoolteachers willing to teach black pupils in the white schools but that public pressure precluded their acting on these sentiments.[59]

By the late 1850s, a concerted campaign by black residents of Providence to integrate the common school system had developed. Discontent with the caste school system, some of the black political leadership that had developed during the 1840s joined forces with the wealthy black entrepreneur George T. Downing and pressed the case for school integration. The integrationists would find themselves pitted against erstwhile allies, black and white, of the 1840s. Their efforts would not succeed until after the Civil War, but even their antebellum failure indicates how far blacks in Providence had come during the previous decade.[60]

A change had occurred in Rhode Island in the late 1840s and during the 1850s. By 1846, naturalized Irish-Americans sought black as well as white support for a measure that would permit them to vote without paying a property tax. During the election of 1848, there was serious competition for the black vote; Whig, Free-Soil, and even Democratic politicians canvassed the black electorate. In that year, the Rhode Island legislature stopped state officers from assisting in the return of fugitive slaves. The Fugitive Slave Law of 1850 had angered many whites in the state, even those not especially noted for previous pro-black sympathies. By the 1850s, the Rhode Island State Anti-Slavery Society was able to meet without encountering the sort of difficulties that abolitionists encountered all too frequently in the 1830s and early 1840s. In 1851, Frederick Douglass was able to address a meeting of that organization in Providence and counsel violent resistance to slave-catchers. He could do this in a city where just a short decade before, abolitionist Abby Kelly had been attacked by a snowball-throwing mob, a city where abolitionists encountered resistance when merely trying to rent rooms.[61]

Even partisan political activity reflected the different atmosphere that existed in the state by the 1850s. The right of black men to vote had survived the election of a Democratic governor in 1851; they did not lose what they had won the decade before once their political adversaries gained power. Later in the decade, the almost accidental election of a black man in Providence to a minor office would again demonstrate that change had occurred. In 1857 Thomas Howland was elected to the office of election warden for Providence's Third Ward. He was not elected because of any great popular sentiment in his favor, nor was he elected because Republicans felt that they needed to reward the loyalty of black voters by electing a black man to a public office, however minor. He was elected because most voters thought they had elected the Third Ward warden on the previous day. Because a change in the election law rendered that election void, a handful of voters were able to put Howland in office the next day. What is most significant is not the peculiar circumstances of Howland's election but the fact that he was able to get a grudging measure of acceptance as he fulfilled his duties for one year. He supervised election activities in the Third Ward, even working with a white deputy who was his subordinate. He was not renominated by the Republicans the following year, and many whites were clearly unhappy with a black man's having even so minor a position of public authority; nonetheless Howland was permitted to serve his term, and to exercise the authority of his office.[62]

These developments were possible because events that had happened in Rhode Island and elsewhere in the nation had caused a change in the attitude toward the state's black population. For the most part that change in attitude could not accurately be described as bringing about any genuine enlightenment on racial matters, but it did represent something of an improvement. The changing attitudes were brought about in part because blacks voted and politicians sought their votes and were less likely to offend potential political supporters. There also grew to be something of a self-congratulatory mood in Rhode Island about its enlightened policies toward the free

Negroes of the state. And especially toward the end of the 1850s, growing antisouthern sectional sentiment made more whites in Rhode Island willing to listen to voices from local black communities. It was against this background that some began to question the continued segregation of schools.

Events elsewhere contributed to the development of school integration sentiment in Providence. Rhode Island's continued support of a black militia company in Providence was noted and envied in free Negro communities elsewhere. Boston black leader William C. Nell mentioned it in his *Colored Patriots of the Ameri can Revolution*. It was also cited by a group of blacks in Boston who tried, unsuccessfully, to get state support for a similar company that they were attempting to form. The national attention that this company received in the antislavery press could not have escaped the attention of the leaders of Providence's black community. It served as one more example of how far they had come since the beginning of the 1840s. On paper the laws of Rhode Island were, with few exceptions, color blind. One of the exceptions was in the field of education.[63]

While Boston blacks were looking at the Providence black militia and wondering why their state could not sponsor a similar organization, they were also comparing their city unfavorably with another city in their home state, New Bedford. New Bedford's schools were integrated, and blacks in Boston wanted to know why schools in their city were not. In 1855, the Massachusetts legislature, dominated by Know-Nothing supporters, passed legislation abolishing segregated schools in the state.[64]

If Boston, why not Providence? Rhode Island law now proclaimed the equality of black and white. As blacks and their white partisans were fond of pointing out, blacks had helped save Rhode Island from mob rule during the Dorr rebellion. Black property holding and taxpaying had increased. A letter to the *Liberator* expressed one of the arguments frequently advanced for school integration:

The colored People of Rhode Island deserve the good opinion and kind feeling of every citizen of the state for their conduct during the recent troublous times of the Dorr excitement in Providence. They promptly volunteered their services for any duty they might be useful in maintaining law and order. Upwards of a hundred of them organized themselves for the purposes of acting as a city guard for the protection of the city and to extinguish fires in the case of their occurrence while the citizens were absent on military duty. The fathers of these people were distinguished for their patriotism and bravery in the war of the revolution, and the Rhode Island colored regiment fought on one occasion until half of their number were slain. There was not a regiment in the service which did more soldierly duty, or showed itself more devotedly patriotic.[65]

George T. Downing was an important figure in Rhode Island's school integration movement. The son of a prosperous black restaurateur in New York City, Downing opened a restaurant in Newport in 1846. In the 1850s he divided his time between a catering business in Providence and a luxury hotel in Newport. In the late 1840s, Downing, who had attended Hamilton College, attempted to enroll his children in Newport's white common schools. He was rebuffed in this attempt. In 1855 he joined forces with Providence's indigenous black leadership. they began the campaign to integrate the schools.[66]

Preliminary organization for the movement took place in 1855. George Henry, a prosperous black gardener who supported the integration effort, revealed in his autobiography the uphill struggle the integrationists had:

In the year of our Lord 1855, I turn my attention to the subject of public school rights. I find myself paying a heavy tax, and my children debarred from attending the schools, for which I was taxed. So a few of us got together and resolved to defend ourselves against such an outrage. Mr. George T. Downing was the leading man in the first part of the campaign.
The first petition was to break up the colored schools, and let the children go into the different ward schools. Upon that I bolted, and declared I could not believe we had any right to break up that school— told him so—and that upon that plank they would whip us, and they did. We were left with not a single plank to stand upon, and all said they would never agree to break up a school that their forefathers worked so hard to establish. So the next year my proposal was to petition the General Assembly that my child should go to school in my own ward, where I pay taxes and vote. So when the petition went in, our opponents had not a plank to stand upon, we swept every plank from under them. . . .
We had a very severe contest, but we were determined never to give

the struggle over till victory was gained. When we started the battle, nine-tenths of the population was against us, ministers and deacons of churches, and what was more grinding to us, two-thirds of the colored population was against us. About the seventh year of the contest, George Head opened his rum shop on South Main street, and invited all colored people who would remonstrate against the bill to come into his place and drink free rum.[67]

The campaign began with a series of appeals on the part of the integrationists to do away with the caste school system. Led by George T. Downing and Ichabod Northup, the desegregation advocates petitioned the general assembly in 1857. Their letter to the general assembly, *Will the General Assembly Put Down Caste Schools*, expressed their desire for a better future for their children:

Our grievance is, that the local school powers of the three places above mentioned [Providence, Bristol and Newport] have given us indifferent school houses, with but partial accommodations as compared with the other school houses: that they have given us indifferent teachers: but aside from all this, even had these parties given us all the accommodation they give others—as good school houses, as good teachers and the like, still would we complain and deny the right of these parties to select us out—set us apart, make us a proscribed class, and thereby cause us to feel that we have separate interests and not alike concerned and interested in whatever pertains to the interest of the State; and thereby cause us to be regarded in the eyes of the community as an inferior, a despised class to be looked down upon; and thus blunt our patriotism—thus impair those noble and manly aspirations that induce a man to strive to be something; to labor on and upward with other men; that induce a parent to say to his child strive, "strive my son, an inviting and honorable field of promotion is before you."[68]

The petitioners went on to detail the inequities of segregated education. They called for equal enforcement of truancy laws, expressing the belief that a vigorous enforcement of such regulations would cause some black parents to be more conscientious about sending their children to school. The appeal to the general assembly complained that the black child had "to go by the school of his ward and district, of his vicinity, at all seasons, in all weathers, from the remotest points to one and a particular

Grammar School." The petition emphasized that black children were barred from the high school even though their parents were taxed for its operation. They also charged that the physical facilities of the two black schools were inferior to those of their white counterparts.[69]

Like Boston school integration proponents in 1855, the Providence integrationists pointed to another city with integrated schools. This time Boston served as the example of racial progress. As part of the petition, George Downing included a letter from Boston school superintendent John D. Philbrick. Philbrick's letter, written in late February 1857, was solicited by Downing. He had written Philbrick on February 16, 1857, and asked him about the progress of school integration in Boston. Philbrick indicated that there were no ill effects resulting from Boston's desegregation. White pupils were not withdrawn by parents protesting integration, and there seemed to be little friction between black and white pupils in the classroom. Philbrick expressed the opinion that "the colored schools in Boston were not disbanded too soon," and he indicated his approval of integrated education by mentioning two black college students who were accepted in otherwise all-white schools.[70]

Realizing that theirs would be an uphill struggle, the integration advocates sought to marshal as much support as possible by assuaging the fears of those who felt that white children would be harmed by common education with black children. In addition to soliciting Philbrick's endorsement, the petitioners presented favorable comments from others involved in Massachusett's newly integrated schools. School officials from Cambridge, Nantucket, New Bedford, and Boston all indicated the success of the abolition of the segregated school system. One of the primary concerns of white opponents of school integration—that some whites would leave the schools if blacks came in—was answered by people in the Boston system who indicated that although a few white parents did withdraw their children, most left their children in the schools. Many of those who withdrew their children later returned them when they discovered the high cost of private education.[71]

Despite the case presented by the proponents of school integration, the cause of desegregation met with strong opposition from whites and a mixture of opposition and ambivalence on the part of many blacks as well. The *Providence Journal* opposed the change and spent a good deal of time attacking George Downing as an outsider fomenting trouble among what the *Journal* saw as an essentially content black population. The *Providence Journal* formerly Whig but now Republican, argued that integration of the schools would drive out rich white children, depriving the schools of their democratic character. It raised the spectre of white girls' being compelled to go to school with black boys and indicated that taxpayers would refuse to support integrated schools. Among its many statements on the subject, the *Journal* denounced the "proposition to abolish the colored schools and force into our public institutions a social equality that does not exist elsewhere."[72]

The campaign to abolish the black schools seems to have met with an ambivalent and sometimes hostile reaction on the part of many black residents of Providence. George Henry indicated that the effort met with the opposition of many blacks. Henry himself, though in favor of school integration, was opposed to the elimination of the Meeting Street and Pond Street schools. The *Providence Journal* frequently assured its readers that black parents were satisfied with the two schools. William J. Brown, one of the major political leaders of the black community, as well as its principal chronicler, failed to mention the school desegregation effort. He signed neither the 1857 petition to the Rhode Island General Assembly, *Will the General Assembly Put Down Caste Schools*, nor the 1859 prointegration statement, *To the Friends of Equal Rights in Rhode Island.* His noninvolvement in the activities of the integrationists stands out in sharp contrast to his leadership role in the political rights efforts of the 1840s and his letter to the *Liberator* supporting integration in 1839.[73]

White intimidation and black fear of losing hard-won gains seem to have contributed to black conservatism regarding school integration. White employers threatened black participants in the integration movement with loss of jobs, in much the same way Whig employers had coerced black workers to the polls a decade before. The petition, *Will the General Assembly Put Down Caste Schools*, charged that many blacks opposed the school integration effort because they feared their employers' retaliation. George Henry said that he was subject to economic pressure because of his prointegration activities. Henry, a gardener employed by different white residents of Providence, was threatened with the loss of several jobs because of his support of school integration.[74]

The petition asserted that although many in the black community were intimidated into supporting continued segregation, the prosperous and better educated in the community were behind the desegregation movement. An examination of the names of those who signed the petition buttresses the point of view that the leaders of the movement were the elite of Providence's free Negro society. Among the signers were George T. Downing, a wealthy caterer; Ichabod Northup, a porter who owned over $3,000 worth of real estate; James M. Cheeves, a gunsmith who owned nearly $4,000 worth of property; and Walter Booth, a laborer who owned nearly $2,000 worth of real estate. By 1859, John T. Waugh, a waiter owning some $1,500 worth of real estate; Ransom Parker, a laborer owning some $1,800 worth of real estate; and George Henry, owner of $3,500 worth of real estate, lent their names to the movement by signing *To the Friends of Equal Rights in Rhode Island*. Of the eleven men who signed *Will the General Assembly Put Down Caste Schools*, four can be identified as major property holders in the Providence black community. Of the twelve who signed *To the Friends of Equal Rights in Rhode Island*, seven can be identified as substantial property holders. It appears that property owners better able to withstand the financial intimidations of white employers spearheaded the drive for integration.[75]

Intimidation was not the only reason for the reticence of many members of the black community regarding the school integration question. Some desired to save the Meeting Street and Pond Street schools, which had received widespread praise and also employed black teachers. For a community constantly trying to assert its dignity and to maintain a semblance of financial well-being, the three black teachers employed by the Providence school board were important. They were in a profession in which few antebellum free Negroes were to be found. They also received steady, relatively high salaries. Many blacks, not satisfied with Downing's and Northup's assurances that integrated schools would not necessarily mean the firing of black teachers, felt it better to maintain the dual system and continue to employ black teachers.[76]

Black and white opposition notwithstanding, the integrationists worked for the cause of a single school system. Early in 1858 the Rhode Island General Assembly failed to pass a measure that would integrate the schools statewide. Later that year, Ichabod Northup pleaded the cause of school integration before the Providence City Council and the Providence School Committee. Northup seems to have had little self-interested reason for pleading the cause of school integration; the schooling for his son, Ichabod, Jr., was over, and the younger Northup had married and was working as a shoemaker. Northup seems to have been motivated primarily by a desire for community betterment.[77]

Northup and others appeared before the Providence School Committee. The committee listened to their arguments. The response was negative. Opponents of school integration claimed benefits for both black and white if segregation continued. One member of the committee agreed that segregated schools were a violation of the racial equality proudly proclaimed by Rhode Island. This member stated that as a state legislator, he would have voted for the abolition of separate black schools, but he felt such a vote inappropriate for a school board member. Thomas M. Clark, Episcopal bishop of Rhode Island and member of the Providence School Committee, vacillated on the issue of integrating Providence's schools. Clark decried separate schools. He saw no evil resulting from the integration of Boston schools. After saying this, he stated his belief that black and white students in Providence would be better off in separate schools. Consistently inconsistent, Bishop Clark then said that if he were black, he would press for the abolition of the caste schools.[78]

It went on that way; the school board members conceded the injustice of the separate school system but said that worse would result with abolition. School board members sought to assuage the petitioners by noting that Providence's black schools enjoyed good reputations, that they were good educational institutions. One argument was that school integration was desirable but inconvenient. The other pointed out the benefits of continued segregation.[79]

The struggle continued. In 1859 school integration was being considered by the state legislature. A petition signed by forty-five black men from Providence arguing against integration helped defeat the measure. The effort would continue until after the Civil War; Rhode Island schools were integrated in 1866. The difficulties and failures of the antebellum school integration movement indicate that profound changes had occurred in Rhode Island race relations.[80] Black petitioners had come a distance from the time a generation before when they could be dismissed with the cry of "Shall a Nigger be allowed to go to polls and tie my vote?" By the late 1850s, these petitioners represented a community of voters, and they were incarnate symbols of forces and ideas that were tearing the country apart. They had a hearing. Attempts were made to assuage their fears, to assure them that the community's children were receiving a good education. Perhaps this unsuccessful campaign most clearly demonstrated their transition from slave to citizen.

Analysis

On one level black political behavior in Providence in the 1840s and 1850s has an obvious explanation. Rejected by the Suffrage party and the Democrats, blacks became Whig stalwarts. On this point the historical record is clear. But is there more? Were there psychological and social factors that should be examined not as alternative hypotheses to the simple historical record but as ancillary explanations? Was there more to the Negro-Whig alliance than the simple events of the early 1840s reveal?

There has been a conflict between the democratic impulse and the ideal of racial egalitarianism for a long time in American society. A quick glance over the pages of an American history text would (or should) reveal Jacksonian-era suffrage extenders vigorously denying the vote to free blacks, early labor organizers setting up white-only unions, southern populists midwifing Jim Crow, New Dealers devising segregated depression-relief programs. The democratic-populist-racist tradition is a long one, including within its ranks Andrew Jackson, Andrew Johnson, Samuel Gompers, "Pitchfork" Ben Tillman, Tom Watson, Woodrow Wilson, Theodore Bilbo, George Wallace, and numerous others.

The earliest political expression of the democratic-racist impulse came in early nineteenth-century New York. From the late eighteenth century on, black voters in New York aligned themselves with the party of their former masters, the Federalist In 1821 Democratic-Republicans under the leadership of Martin Van Buren pressed for black disenfranchisement, charging that black voters were the captives of their Federalist former masters A compromise was worked out that set up the $250 freehold requirement for black voters and universal suffrage for whites.[81]

And what of this charge, made during the genesis of the nation's political system, that blacks were the political tools of the elite, their former masters? This charge was to be repeated over and over again in American history. It would be expressed by those who developed political machines among poor and working-class white groups, political machines that routinely bought and sold votes for concrete favors. This belief, instrumental in curtailing black voting rights in the antebellum North, became a rationale for the disenfranchisement of black voters in the late nineteenth- and early twentieth-century South.[82]

In Anglo-American culture, voters often have cast ballots because of personal loyalties or in return for tangible, individual rewards. Frequently the patron, whose combination of favors, friendliness, and threats brought a sufficient number of clients to the polls, decided elections. This was part of the United States' political legacy from Britain. Historian Wallace Notestein's description of election practices in seventeenth-century England bears a marked resemblance to the methods used to persuade black voters in both the African Governors' elections and the general elections in the 1840s:

If a member of one of those families sought election, the other family was likely to throw its support to a rival candidate, possibly to one of its own connection. In any case there emerged usually two sets of candidates with their arrayed supporters. Those supporters would gather in for the great day and might be given hospitality. They would include many forty-shilling freeholders, who had the right to vote. But one of the candidates might bring in a lot of substantial looking yeomen. Who was to say offhand that they were not forty-shilling freeholders.[83]

Blacks in the Northeast were among the first Americans to join in this political tradition. The African Governors' elections of the eighteenth century were socializing rituals. Not only were Africans introduced to Anglo-American election practice, they were shown how a lower-class voter was expected to make his decision. The patron sponsored a candidate, his slave, and that candidate won because of the entertainments and favors his master could bestow on the electorate, the slave population.

Integration into the political culture did not end with the African Governors' elections. One of the cases that we have of a black man voting in Rhode Island before the disenfranchisement of 1822 indicates that the continuity between the acculturation to Anglo-American electoral practices during slavery and actual black voting in the late eighteenth and early nineteenth centuries may have been quite strong. One Primus Collins was a black voter in Rhode Island before disenfranchisement. He had previously been an African Governor when he was a slave to Colonel William Richmond of Little Compton, Rhode Island. When Richmond freed Collins, he gave him a plot of land large enough to allow Collins to attain freeman status. Compton then pressured a reluctant election official to allow Collins to exercise his suffrage right. This is not the only case of strong links that originated in slavery influencing the right of a black person to vote. By some quirk of New Jersey law, slaves may have voted in late eighteenth- and early nineteenth-century New Jersey. At least one account tells of a master who carried several of his slaves to the poll in a wagon, bringing them to vote, presumably for his candidate.[84]

Early black voters, those freed in the late eighteenth and early nineteenth centuries, voted Federalist, arousing the Democratic ire, because it was with their former Federalist masters that they had personal contact. Consider a slave freed in New York, the state we have the most information about, in the late eighteenth century. As that century ends and the new one begins, he starts to vote. One thing can be immediately de-

duced from this set of circumstances is that this freedman is
fortunate. He, a former slave, has managed to acquire enough
property to vote, something many of his white contemporaries
have not done. It is not unreasonable to assume that a significant
number of former slaves in a position to vote had help from
their former masters in acquiring property. Perhaps, like some
slaves in Newport and Providence, Rhode Island, they had been
educated by their masters; maybe, like Primus Collins, they
received gifts of property upon manumission; maybe their former masters became their employers. In any event, as the nineteenth century began, enough black voters stood ready to play
forty-shilling freeholder to their upper-class ex-masters' English
lord. Gratitude for tangible benefits bestowed on a family caused
heads of households to vote with their benefactors.

The emerging urban elite in the Northeast was Federalist. If
they could not be identified as proponents of democratic-egali-
tarianism, many nonetheless were sympathetic to black rights.
Federalist architect and champion of propertied suffrage, Alexander Hamilton, was also active in the New York Manumission
Society. Federalists seemed to be the least opposed to black suffrage, perhaps feeling that any person possessing sufficient
property to qualify for the vote was worthy of that privilege.
In early nineteenth-century New York, the alliance began.[85]

Historian Lee Benson asserts that the hypothesis that ex-
Federalists became Whigs is untested and perhaps untrue. However true this may be generally, the move from Federalist to
Whig for black voters is clear. A target of the Democratic party,
New York black voters stayed with the Whigs. A sizable portion
of New York Whigs upheld the Federalist tradition of supporting black voting rights.[86]

This background, New York history, and of course the African Governors' elections were all part of the general knowledge
of Providence blacks as they pushed for suffrage in the late 1830s
and early 1840s. Alexander Crummell, a leader among Providence
black suffrage advocates, had recently come from New York
where he had fought unsuccessful battles against New York Democrats in an attempt to abolish the $250 freehold requirement for
black voters. If by no other way, black suspicion of Democrats
came to Providence with Crummell. Still they went to the Suffrage Association first. Only after their rebuff did they pick up

the pattern that had been operating in New York for at least two generations.[87]

Something besides the Suffrage Association's rejection of black voters and the legacy of conflict bequeathed poor whites and blacks from New York needs to be considered. How did the black activist who pushed for suffrage extension and later for school rights view himself and his community? What were his personal and group aspirations? Did these contribute to the conflict between black and laboring white and to the black-Whig connection?

If the writings of Providence's black political and social leaders document anything, they document a search for status, a desire for recognition of black achievement and respectability. From colonial times, the black population had been labeled as part of Providence's deviant underclass. Nineteenth-century observers detected social pathologies in Providence's black community and were quick to make the generalization that Negroes were "an ignorant and degraded class." The people whose abuse of their children led white philanthropists to form the Providence Asylum and Shelter for Colored Children, the drunkards and criminals, became a psychological burden on the rest of the black population.[88]

So the search for respectability and for vindication began, first with church and school and later with the temperance society. Property holding, sobriety, church attendance, education, marrying late after one had acquired enough income to support a family—these characteristics took on increased virtue for the stable black laborers and mechanics of Providence. These things put a social distance between respectable black families and the black deviants they were all too often identified with and, indeed, the white rowdies they were all too often forced to live among.

The search spread to politics. Even in arguing their case to the laborers and mechanics of the Suffrage Association, black leaders emphasized achievement and respectability. To be sure, an appeal to republican principles was made. The petition to the Suffrage Association made by Northup and his associates reiterated the stability, property holding, and support of education that existed in the black community. While Suffrage Association leaders like mechanic Seth Luther felt it only necessary to appeal to democratic ideals, Northup had to make the case for acceptability. Luther's group did not suffer from the presumption of deviance. Northup's did.

There was another critical difference between Luther and Northup. Their workaday lives could not have been much different. Luther was a wheelwright. Northup tried small business; later he became a laborer. Yet Northup was near the top of black society, Luther near the bottom of white. Discrimination and lack of wealth gave Providence blacks little opportunity for occupational advancement. Except for a few ministers, a professional class was nonexistent. In this respect Providence blacks had less opportunity than their contemporaries in cities like Boston, New York, Philadelphia, and Rochester, New York, where size and circumstance often permitted a few blacks to become lawyers, doctors, and journalists.

Most blacks in Providence were low and semiskilled workers. A few managed to become independent businessmen, shoemakers, barbers, and the like. There were few substantial property holders in the black community. For these reasons, status could scarcely be based on wealth and occupation. To be sure, the ministers, who also served as the community's educators, were respected and were clearly community leaders. John W. Lewis and his temperance activities had an enormous impact before he left for Concord, New Hampshire. But except for the ministers and of course an exception (like George Downing), black leadership came from among the laborers, mechanics, and small shopkeepers of black Providence. A laborer who had read of Andrew Jackson's exhortation to the free people of color during the Battle of New Orleans, a well-read barber, an intensely religious shoemaker—these were the sorts of people that achieved high status in the black community.

So what of this search for respectability and the respective statuses of the Seth Luthers and Ichabod Northups? These are important, for they indicate that the outlook of the black leaders may have been different, indeed perhaps more aristocratic than those of the white workingmen whom they first attempted to join. Decades of contact, malevolent and benevolent, with upper-class whites, combined with the quest for status and respectability, made black values and the black struggle for suffrage an experience different from the Suffrage Association's odyssey.

In this light, we may turn to two different explanations for black affinity for the Whig party. The first is the simple story of Suffrage party rejection. The second is that Whig affiliation satisfied a need for status, for recognition of group respectability. Black movement to the Law and Order party preceded that organization's actual championing of black suffrage. As was the case during the Revolution, the War of 1812, and indeed in later national crises, black people felt that loyalty and sacrifice would vindicate the search for acceptability. In the case of Providence, that faith was partially affirmed.

Providence and the nation had come a distance from the days when Venture Smith and an Irish servant had hatched their escape plot in southern Rhode Island. Their figurative, if not their literal, descendants no longer sought common goals. Caught between competing forces, one that excluded because of caste, the other because of class, they chose sides. It is a tragic legacy we still share.

Notes

1. J. Stanley Lemons and Michael A. McKenna, "Reenfranchisement of Rhode Island Negroes," *Rhode Island History* 30 (February 1971): 3-4; *Liberator,* October 18, 1839.

2. Lemons and McKenna, "Reenfranchisement."

3. Ibid.; Arthur Mowry, *The Dorr War* (Providence: Preston and Round, 1901); George M. Dennison, *The Dorr War* (Lexington: University of Kentucky Press, 1976); Marvin E. Gettleman, *The Dorr Rebellion* (New York: Random House, 1973).

4. Brown, *The Life of William J. Brown,* p. 86.

5. Lemons and McKenna, "Reenfranchisement," p. 7; Seth Luther, *An Address on the Right of Free Suffrage* (Providence: S. R. Weeden, 1833), passim.

6. Luther, *Address.*

7. Lemons and McKenna, "Reenfranchisement," p. 7; Dan King, *The Life and Times of Thomas Wilson Dorr* (Boston, 1859), pp. 284-89; Gettleman, *Dorr Rebellion,* pp. 12-19.

8. King, *Life and Times of Dorr.*

9. Jacob Frieze, *A Concise History of the Efforts to Obtain an Extension of Suffrage in Rhode Island* (Providence: B. F. Moore, 1842), p. 31.

10. *New Age and Constitutional Advocate*, November 20, December 4, 18, 25, 1840, January 22, February 5, 1841.

11. Ibid., April 23, 1841; *Providence Journal*, September 15, 1841.

12. *Providence Journal*, September 15, 1841.

13. Ibid.

14. Ibid., September 17, 1841.

15. Ibid., September 27, 1841.

16. *New Age and Constitutional Advocate*, October 22, 1841; U.S. Congress, House, Select Committee Report No. 546, "Interference in the Internal Affairs of Rhode Island," pp. 111-13.

17. *New Age and Constitutional Advocate*, October 22, 1841.

18. Gettleman, *Dorr Rebellion*, p. 209.

19. *Liberator*, October 14, 1842; Lemons and McKenna, "Reenfranchisement," p. 9; *New Age and Constitutional Advocate*, December 17, 1841.

20. Lemons and McKenna, "Reenfranchisement"; Frieze, *Concise Histo* p. 28.

21. *Liberator*, August 19, 1842; Lemons and McKenna, "Reenfranchisement," p. 12; *Liberator*, January 21, 1842; *Providence Daily Journal*, January 1, 1842.

22. Lemons and McKenna, "Reenfranchisement," pp. 11-12.

23. Brown, *Life of Brown*, pp. 173-74.

24. Ibid.

25. Ibid.

26. Ibid.; William C. Nell, *The Colored Patriots of the Revolution* (Boston: R. F. Wallcut, 1855).

27. *Providence Journal*, September 16, 1842, black men voted in that Law and Order convention. The convention put a referendum before the voters in November that would permit black suffrage. The measure won by a wide margin, 3,157 to 1,004, for three reasons: the provision was worded in such a way that those opposing black suffrage were required to insert the word *white* into the document; many Suffrage party sympathizers boycotted the election; and blacks were allowed to vote in the referendum. Because there were at least 670 black men over the age of twenty-one and probably well over 700, the eligibility of black men to participate in the referendum contributed significantly to the success of the measure. See Gettleman, *Dorr Rebellion*, pp. 145, 148; U.S. Census, 1840 (published).

28. Lee Benson, *The Concept of Jacksonian Democracy* (Princeton, N.J.: Princeton University Press, 1961), pp. 315, 318.

29. Brown, *Life of Brown*, pp. 156-68.

30. The terms *Whig* and *Law and Order* parties are being somewhat loosely interchanged here, though strictly speaking the Law and Order party was a coalition containing both Whigs and conservative Democrats.

The Whigs were the dominant group in the coalition, and black voters stayed with that dominant Whig group as the Law and Order coalition dissolved during the 1840s. Also during that decade black voters cast their vote for the Whig candidates in the national elections while voting for the Law and Order candidates during state contests.

31. Frieze, *Concise History*, pp. 30-31.

32. *National Anti-Slavery Standard*, April 27, 1843; *Liberator*, October 18, 1844.

33. Brown, *Life of Brown*, pp. 149-151. Estimates of potential black voters are taken from the U.S. censuses of 1840, 1850, and 1860. The 1840 censuses indicated that there were 670 black men over the age of twenty-four and 388 men between the ages of ten and twenty-four. The 1850 census listed 1,027 black men over the age of twenty. The 1860 census listed 1,014 black men over the age of twenty. The election data were taken from statistics compiled by the University of Michigan's Interuniversity Consortium on Political and Social Research, United States Historical Election Returns, 1788-1977 (hereafter referred to as ICPSR). The Providence city census of 1845 confirms the accuracy of Brown's estimate that there were between 300 and 400 black voters in this period. That census indicated there were 349 black men over the age of twenty-four and 101 black men between the ages of ten and twenty-four in the city.

34. To appreciate how effective the $134 freehold requirement was in limiting the numbers of foreign-born voters, it should be borne in mind that according to the U.S. Census of 1850, a man working in one of the Rhode Island textile mills received an average wage of about $20 per month and probably did not receive even this on a sustained basis. The freehold requirement was such an effective screen that although the 1860 census listed a foreign-born population of 37,394 and a black population of 3,952, the number of blacks eligible to vote was near 1,000, while the number of foreign-born voters was only 1,260 in 1865. See Peter J. Coleman, *The Transformation of Rhode Island, 1790-1860* (Providence: Brown University Press, 1963).

35. The election figures for the Providence results in the gubernatorial elections of 1843 and 1845 were taken from Gettleman's estimates. See Gettleman, *Dorr Rebellion*, appendix B, p. 235. His figures are at a slight variance with those reported by ICPSR. For the statewide results in the 1843 election, Gettleman reported 8,990 votes for Fenner and 7,427 votes for Carpenter. For the 1845 election, he reported 7,394 votes for Fenner and 7,587 votes for Jackson. See table 3-1 for the ICPSR tallies. The figures for the 1844 presidential election are taken from ICPSR.

36. Brown, *Life of Brown*, p. 157; *National Anti-Slavery Standard*, April 27, 1843.

37. Brown, *Life of Brown*, pp. 157-58.

38. The definition of *lower class* here is not an economic one. Most of the black men who voted in antebellum Providence would have been poor laborers. The term *lower class* is used here as an indication of social attitudes and habits, receptivity toward education, church going—what we call the work ethic and the like. The lower-class voters whom the Whigs were anxious to make sure did not fall into the hands of the Democrats were the disreputable element of the community whom people like Brown were constantly asserting did not represent the community.

39. Brown, *Life of Brown*, p. 159.

40. Ibid.; Nell, *Colored Patriots*.

41. *North Star*, September 1, 1841.

42. Eric Foner, *Free Soil, Free Labor, Free Men: The Ideology of the Republican Party Before the Civil War* (New York: Oxford University Press, 1970), pp. 152-53.

43. *North Star*, August 25, September 1, 1848.

44. Ibid., September 1, 1848.

45. Ibid.

46. Fox, "Negro Vote in Old New York"; Benson, *The Concept of Jacksonian Democracy*, p. 179; *North Star*, August 25, 1848. Historian Lee Benson estimates the black voting population in New York to have been around 1,000 in the 1840s. In 1848 black abolitionist S. R. Ward estimated that there were between 3,000 and 4,000 black voters in New York State *North Star*, August 25, 1848.

47. *National Anti-Slavery Standard*, April 27, 1843; *Liberator*, October 18, 1844; *North Star*, September 1, 1848.

48. Brown, *Life of Brown*, p. 158.

49. *Providence Journal*, October 30, 1848.

50. Ibid., November 4, 1848.

51. Ibid., November 6, 1848.

52. Brown, *Life of Brown*, p. 161.

53. *Liberator*, December 8, 1848; ICPSR.

54. Brown, *Life of Brown*, p. 158.

55. *Liberator*, October 18, 1839.

56. Thomas B. Stockwell, *A History of Public Education in Rhode Island* (Providence: Providence Press Co., 1876).

57. *City Document No. 2: Annual Report of the School Committee of the City of Providence* (Providence: Knowles, Anthony & Co., 1854), pp. 12-16.

58. Ibid.; *Will the General Assembly Put Down Caste Schools* (Providence, 1857).

59. *Liberator*, October 18, 1839.

60. Lawrence Grossman, "George T. Downing and Desegregation of

Rhode Island Public Schools, 1855-1866," *Rhode Island History* 36, no. 4 (November 1977): 99-105; *Liberator,* February 20, April 17, 1857.

61. *Petition of Henry J. Duff and Others for an Alteration of the State Constitution* (Providence: M. B. Young's Press, 1846), p. 2; *Liberator,* February 11, 1848, November 14, 1851.

62. Robinson, *Blacks in Nineteenth Century Rhode Island,* p. 92; John Howland, "Thomas Howland and His Portrait" (address before the Rhode Island Historical Society, n.d. [nineteenth century]).

63. Nell, *Colored Patriots; Liberator,* September 14, 1855.

64. *Report of the Boston School Committee* (Boston, 1855); James Oliver Horton and Lois E. Horton, *Black Bostonians: Family Life and Community Struggle in the Antebellum North* (New York: Holmes and Meir, 1979), p. 75.

65. *Liberator,* February 20, 1857.

66. Grossman, "Downing and Desegregation"; Charles A. Battle, *Negroes on the Island of Rhode Island* (Newport, 1932).

67. George Henry, *Life of George Henry, Together with a Brief History of the Colored People in America* (Providence: H. I. Gould & Co., 1894), pp. 67-68.

68. *Will the General Assembly Put Down Caste Schools,* p. 3.

69. Ibid.

70. Ibid., p. 11. Boston schools were integrated in 1855.

71. Ibid., pp. 9-10.

72. *Providence Journal,* January 23, 26, 1858.

73. Henry, *Life of Henry,* pp. 67-58; *Providence Journal,* January 26, February 3, May 29, 1858; Brown, *Life of Brown; Will the General Assembly Put Down Caste Schools; To the Friends of Equal Rights in Rhode Island* (Providence, 1859); *Liberator,* October 18, 1839.

74. *Will the General Assembly Put Down Caste Schools,* p. 6; Henry, *Life of Henry,* pp. 66-69.

75. *Will the General Assembly Put Down Caste Schools; To the Friends of Equal Rights in Rhode Island;* U.S. Census, 1850 (manuscript); U.S. Census, 1860 (manuscript).

76. *Will the General Assembly Put Down Caste Schools,* p. 6.

77. *Liberator,* January 29, 1858; U.S. Census, 1850 (manuscript); U.S. Census, 1860 (manuscript).

78. *Liberator,* January 29, 1858. Bishop Clark was a conservative on questions of race and slavery, though he was also something of an admirer of the black community in Providence. In a sermon delivered in Grace Church in Providence in 1860, he counseled northerners to be patient with southerners and the institution of slavery. He considered slavery as a school for civilization. He then proceeded to point out how Rhode Island slavery had produced a model free Negro population in Providence.

See Thomas M. Clark, *The State of the Country, a Sermon Delivered in Grace Church Providence* (Providence, 1860). Clark was also a colonization advocate. Henry, *Life of Henry*, p. 70.

79. *Liberator*, January 29, 1858.

80. Grossman, "Downing and Desegregation," p. 102; *Providence Journal*, March 4, 9, 1859; Henry, *Life of Henry*, p. 60.

81. Benson, *Concept of Jacksonian Democracy*, p. 10.

82. C. Vann Woodward, *The Strange Career of Jim Crow* (New York: Oxford University Press, 1957), pp. 53-65, 80.

83. Wallace Notestein, *The English People on the Eve of Colonization* (New York: Harper, 1954), pp. 208-9. See also Basil Duke Henning, Archibald S. Foord, and Barbara L. Mathias, *Crises in English History, 1066-1945* (New York: Holt, Rinehart & Co., 1964). In this collection of documents, there is the lament of one English nobleman discussing smaller freeholders selling their votes for a pot of ale (p. 356).

84. Benjamin Franklin Wilbur, *Little Compton Families*, p. 520; Marion Thompson Wright, "Negro Suffrage in New Jersey, 1776-1875," *Journal of Negro History* 33 (April 1948): 173-74.

85. Fox, "Negro Vote in Old New York."

86. Benson, *Concept of Jacksonian Democracy*, p. 180.

87. Lemons and McKenna, "Reenfranchisement," p. 4.

88. Providence Association for the Benefit of Colored Children, *Annual Reports 1-12* (Providence, 1840-1851).

OCCUPATION, STATUS, AND POPULATION

4

Barbers and laborers represented the community in its political struggles. The history of the community is revealed to us in the writings of a shoemaker. The humble circumstances of many of the town's more prominent blacks testify to the limited opportunities for blacks in antebellum Providence. Surviving narrative sources also document the economic difficulties of black Providence.

By combining literary sources with censuses, city directories, and probate records, we can get a picture of the economic and social conditions of blacks in mid-nineteenth-century Providence. This chapter is primarily concerned with the occupational structure of the Providence black community. Questions to be answered include: In what occupations were blacks engaged? From what occupations were blacks absent or excluded? Which occupations offered blacks the greatest chances for economic success and perhaps social and political leadership as well? This chapter will also look at certain distinctions in the Providence Negro community—the black-mulatto distinction, distinctions based on geographic origins, and the male-female distinction—to see if any of these differences may have influenced an individual's occupation or economic success.

The second concern of this chapter will be a description of the population. Just looking at the community's occupational

structure gives some sense of what the population was like,
but the sources can tell more. They can provide glimpses of
day-to-day relations between people of different races. They
also reveal literacy, institutionalization, family patterns, population fertility, pauperism, and patterns of property holding, in-
dicators that give a basis for comparing the black and white
populations. These measures reflect the quality of the lives
of the Providence black community, and they also provide a
framework against which the social and occupational prejudices
the community faced may be assessed.

Blacks as a percentage of Providence's population had steadily
decreased since 1790. In 1790 there were 475 blacks, 7.4 percent of the 6,380 people who lived in Providence. By 1865,
that percentage had shrunk to 3.1 percent, or 1,711 blacks in
a population of 54,595. Between 1790 and 1865 the growth
rate for the white population averaged 3 percent per year,
while the rate for the black population was 1.7 percent per
year. Between 1850 and 1860 the black population's rate of
growth fell drastically. The black population went from 1,499
to 1,537, a rate of growth of 0.25 percent per year. During
the same period, the white population grew from 41,513 to
50,666, a growth rate of 2 percent per year. The drastic decline
in the black growth rate during this period and the less drastic
decline in the white growth rate might be partially attributed to
the depression of 1857 that hurt textile manufacturing and
whaling in Providence. This depression destroyed the Providence whaling industry and may have contributed to the slow
rate of growth among Providence blacks during the 1850s. The
federal censuses show a decrease in the number of black mariners
during that decade; the 1850 census lists forty black mariners,
while the 1860 census lists twenty-seven.[1]

These figures show a larger rate of growth for the white than
the black population, and one possible explanation clearly
would be European and Canadian immigration. But we should
approach these figures and any tentative conclusions with great
caution. While the overall figures from 1790 to 1865 indicate
that the percentage of blacks in Providence's population decline
and that the growth rate of the black population was less than
that of the white population, the figures from 1860 to 1865

indicate a larger growth rate for the black population (2.16 percent per year) than the white population (0.86 percent per year). The migration of black people from the South during the Civil War probably contributed to this increase. It is also likely that at least part of this increase, revealed by the Rhode Island census of 1865, might be attributed to fugitive slaves who remained hidden during previous censuses but who allowed themselves to be counted in 1865, after national emancipation. The question of the exact size of the fugitive slave population in Providence and other northern cities is one that bears further exploration. It could hold the key to a possible underenumeration of antebellum black populations.[2]

Different sex ratios and marriage patterns also help explain the different growth rates for the white and black populations. In 1865 females constituted 53.7 percent of the white population, 58.3 percent of the black population, 59.8 percent of the population born in Ireland, and 52.9 percent of the native-born American population as a whole.

These differences were not just an accident of the 1865 state census. The white sex ratios had been virtually even throughout the antebellum period, while the black ratios showed significant differences during the same period. The 1825 city census indicated that males were only 40.2 percent of the black population, while they were 49.5 percent of the white population. In 1845 men and boys were 41.4 percent of the black population and 49.3 percent of the white. The 1855 census shows that the disparity continued; the black population was 41.2 percent male, the white population 48.1 percent male.[3]

Evidence from the federal censuses of 1850 and 1860 suggests that economic forces drove enough black men away from Providence to account for the disparity in the sex ratios. In both censuses, the male population was roughly equal to the female population among those who were under twenty; the 1850 census showed that males accounted for 49 percent of blacks under twenty in Providence County; in 1860 males under twenty were 50 percent. Both censuses indicated that the sexual imbalances appeared in the adult populations. Men were 42 percent of black adults in 1850, 43 percent in 1860, suggesting that black men left Providence hoping to find work elsewhere. A number undoubtedly worked as seamen on whaling and merchant vessels. If they worked on ships based in Providence, their names should have been recorded at the custom house, and they should have been accounted for in the various local, state, and federal enumerations. Probably a number sought to ply their maritime skills in other New England seaports, and those men probably were more likely not to be counted than those who worked on ships based in Providence. In any event the data suggest that a significant number of men left the city, probably in search of work elsewhere. This was a pattern that seems to have been true in other black communities in northern cities at the time.[4]

This sexual imbalance doubtless contributed to the lesser rate of increase among blacks in Providence. In a community that so fervently espoused rather conservative social values, this paucity of men probably meant that considerable numbers of women remained celibate for large portions of their lives. This imbalance also hampers our ability to make accurate inferences about family structure. There are inherent difficulties in trying to determine family ties from the 1850 and 1860 censuses. Neither census specifically indicated family relationships. Instead inferences have to be made from last names and ages; some erroneous judgments are inevitable. Both censuses indicate that the overwhelming majority of black households with children were stable households with fathers heading the families. Of the 209 families that had children in 1850, 164, or a little more than 78 percent of them, were headed either by fathers alone or fathers and mothers. By 1860 that percentage had dipped somewhat; a little more than 76 percent (159 families) were headed by fathers or both parents. These figures suggest high rates of family stability, comparable to those found in black populations in other cities at the time and even higher than the rates found today. The number and percentage of female-headed households was probably even smaller than these figures indicate. The large population of men who were looking for work outside of Providence invariably would have included men who had left their families in the city. This population would have included men who had by no means deserted their families; instead they kept in regular contact with their wives and children, sending home such money as they could. The increase in the percentage of female-headed households between 1850 and 1860 is convincing testimony of the effect of economic forces on household structure. Hardships brought about by the depression of 1857 doubtless influenced a number of family men to leave Providence in search of better economic opportunity elsewhere.[5]

The parents from the different kinds of families sent their children to school. Census figures confirm the writings of Brown, Northup, and the others that the community placed a high value on education. Of those who were over the age of twenty, better than 94 percent were literate. Those born out of state were disproportionately represented among those in the community who could neither read nor write; thirty-six of the forty-seven black adults who were illiterate were born in states other than Rhode Island. Blacks in Providence were doing somewhat better, in terms of literacy, than black people in other parts of the state; the literacy rate for blacks statewide was roughly 91 percent. If the 1865 state census is a good measure, the black communities in Providence had an appreciably greater percentage of people who were able to read and write than did the Irish immigrant population. That population, statewide, was 73 percent literate. The native white population was better than 99 percent literate during this period. Clearly the writers who stressed the community's concern for education and those who praised the Meeting and Pond Street schools were reflecting real developments. This might also help explain the relatively conservative behavior of the community during the school integration effort.

Still these figures should not blind us to the relative educational deprivations suffered by Providence's black community. Blacks had a lower literacy level than their native-born white counterparts. Also it should be remembered that the term *literate* covered a wide range of skill levels, including those who could barely sign their names. Blacks in Providence were of course doing remarkably well compared to black people elsewhere, but compared to their white counterparts their educational horizons were still limited.[6]

One of the perennial problems faced by men like William J. Brown, Alfred Niger, and Ichabod Northup was the charge

that the black community was a dangerous community, "a
degraded class of persons." Every recorded public action of
these men was, in part, an attempt to counteract this image.
An analysis of the federal census of 1860 indicates that the
combined effects of discrimination and poverty helped produce
a higher rate of institutionalization for blacks than for the
population as a whole. While the rate of institutionalization
by no means tells the whole story, it can give us some clue as
to whether harsh conditions brought about undesirable results
in the black community.

The census of 1860 shows 21 black children in the Providence
Reform School. Six black convicts were in the county jail. Seven
black paupers were in the Dexter asylum for the poor. The state
census of 1865 shows 169 institutionalized paupers in Providence and 107 convicts. We see that 1 in 220 blacks was institutionalized as a pauper as opposed to 1 in 330 in the population
as a whole. The contrast is even starker when we compare rates
of institutionalization for crime; overall, 1 in 510 was held for
criminal activity. For blacks, if we combine those in reform
school with the 6 adult convicts, we get 1 in 57 in correctional
institutions. If we just count the 6 adult convicts, we get a rate
of 1 in 256. If we combine paupers and those held for criminal
activity, we find that in 1865 overall 1 in 198 was in institutions.
The black rate in 1860 was 1 in 45. Comparing these two sample
and assuming no staggering differences occurring in those five
years, the connection between race and institutionalization was
probably highly significant.[7]

Of course, such figures by no means tell the whole story. The
rate of black pauperism seems relatively low. The 1865 census
did not specify how many of the paupers were Irish or French
Canadian immigrants, two groups that it would probably make
more sense to contrast the black population with instead of the
population as a whole. Such a contrast might well reveal that
the black population was better off than these two other workin
class populations in this regard, or such a comparison might reveal a greater reluctance to admit black paupers to charitable institutions. Also, over 79 percent of blacks incarcerated for break
ing the law were children. There was a sharp increase in the incarceration of children and youth between 1850 and 1860. Ac-

cording to the 1850 census four black persons under twenty-one were in the county jail for various offenses. They constituted one-third of blacks in prison in 1850, including three adult prisoners in the state prison. By 1860, the city had opened the Providence Reform School, and the number of imprisoned juveniles had risen to twenty-one. Several possible explanations might be advanced for this increase. Fifteen of the twenty-one were incarcerated for theft or vagrancy, a possible indication that the economic conditions that the 1857 depression had generated caused a number of black children to turn to crime to survive. The fact that the Providence Reform School was not open in 1850 but was in operation in 1860 also probably contributed to the increase in the incarceration of black children. Providence officials who desired to cure what they felt were dangerous tendencies among blacks may have regarded the reform school as an opportunity to mold the ways of the black youth, to prevent what they saw as a tendency for them to join society's dangerous classes. That may have accounted for a high incarceration rate, a rate probably higher than that found among white youths. When one sees higher rates of deviance in a community previously labeled so by the larger society, it is always good to be aware of the possibility that a self-fulfilling prophecy may be at work.

Occupation, Property, and Social Structure

Blacks found it difficult to break out of menial occupations. Black and white observers noted that black poverty helped form a deviant underclass of illiterate, marginally employed people who engaged in criminal behavior. Still, as black activists pointed out, some persevered, acquired property, and engaged in other than menial occupations, despite formidable barriers.

The 1850 and 1860 manuscript censuses show that most blacks in Providence engaged in menial occupations; they were porters, servants, laborers, laundresses, waiters, teamsters, sextons, gardeners, painters, hostlers, cooks, draymen, stevedores, and other unskilled workers.[8] A number of black people have no occupations listed. Many of these were doubtless casual, unskilled laborers who went from menial task to menial task, unable to count on regular employment, eking out a living from day to day. There were a handful of professionals. They, along with small businessmen such as shoemakers, bakers, and grocers, managed to rise above the "hewer of wood and drawer of water" status to which most blacks were relegated.[9]

Blacks were absent from most of the great and minor professions in antebellum Providence. Seventy-five percent of the occupations listed in the Providence census of 1855 had no black practitioners; these occupations employed roughly 30 percent of Providence's work force. Some of these absences can be attributed to chance. There was one phrenologist in Providence, and he happened to be white. One card maker is noted in the 1855 census. Other occupations that had few enough practitioners to make black absence probable included corset makers, caulkers, the town's one gas inspector and one hosemaker, the razor grinder, the two tube makers, among others. Given that blacks were 2.9 percent of the population in 1855, black absence in occupations that employed only a handful of people is hardly surprising.[10]

Blacks were conspicuously absent from two types of occupations: the major professional and entrepreneurial ones. There were no black lawyers, druggists, or newspaper editors. None were listed among the manufacturers, merchants, college professors, or dentists. Poverty, situation, and discrimination contributed to the black absence from these fields. Lack of capital ensured black absence from major business activity. Providence's relatively small size made a black newspaper unlikely. And, of course, racial discrimination also contributed to the black absence from the more elite sectors of Providence's economy.

While black absence from elite occupations in Providence may be attributed to a variety of causes, it seems hard to explain black absence from another class of occupations in any but racial terms. As was the case throughout the North, there was a severe underrepresentation of blacks in the industries that developed in Providence in the nineteenth century. No blacks were counted among the general factory operatives, even though 968 persons were employed in that field. Considering that the black population consisted largely of unskilled workers, the black absence in such a field is hard to explain except as a re-

sult of racial discrimination. Black absence from other manufacturing occupations buttresses the idea that the newer enterprises managed to exclude blacks on a fairly systematic basis.[11]

Black workers, with some exceptions, worked in older occupations, carry-overs from the eighteenth century. Rhode
Island's industrial revolution, which brought textile factories,
ironworking, and other manufacturing concerns to the city,
had bypassed the black community. Blacks were still heavily
engaged in personal service occupations, a clear holdover from
the slave era. They were also mariners, another area in which
they could find employment during the eighteenth century. Of
553 blacks with specifically named occupations listed in the
1860 census, only seven seem to have held jobs that were products of the development of industry in nineteenth-century
Providence. A conservative appraisal of the 15,841 workers
listed in the 1855 census indicates that roughly 2,600 of them
worked in jobs related to the new industrialism. Black workers
were severely underrepresented in this industrial labor force; only
7 black workers worked in what appear to have been factory jobs.[12]

Despite occupational discrimination and low and often irregular wages, a number of black people in Providence acquired
remarkably large amounts of property. If the Providence census
marshal for 1860 caught everything, 53 blacks owned significant
amounts of property in the city that year. As there were some
450 or so households that had blacks, that meant that nearly
88 percent of black households were without appreciable
amounts of property. Even among the property owners there
were wide variations. The poorest of the Negro property owners
was a forty-year-old black coachman; he owned $30 worth of
personal property. Manuel Fenner, a fifty-six-year-old veterinarian
and horse farrier, was the richest member of the community; he
owned $5,000 worth of real and $500 worth of personal property.
Among the 53, the median size property holding was about $900.
(See figure 4-1.) The patterns of property holding revealed by
the 1860 census show a surprising lack of connection between occupation and education on the one hand and property
holding on the other. Table 4-1 provides a list of black people
who held real property valued at over $500 in 1860.

Education or membership in the learned professions did not

Figure 4-1

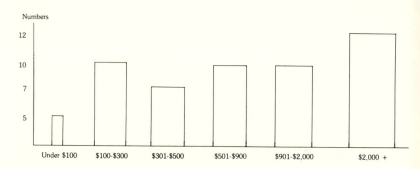

Size of Property Holdings by Providence Blacks, 1860

SOURCE: U.S. Census, 1860.

NOTE: The range is from $30 to $5,500. The median is $900.

help one acquire property. Every one of these major property holders except Manuel Fenner worked as a manual laborer; most were unskilled; a few had managed to open independent businesses. Most of these people left little record of their activities. With the exception of the political activists and a few others, the economic activities of those who acquired property have to be deduced from various government records. Tax lists for Providence go back to 1829 and provide some clue to the processes of property acquisition among Providence blacks. The records indicate a 305 percent growth in total property held by Providence blacks between the years 1829 and 1860. The total real property holding of Providence blacks in 1829 was $22,800; the total in 1860 was $57,090. Between 1829 and 1860 the value of all property held by the black community increased at a rate of roughly 3.7 percent per year.[13]

Those who acquired property had a marked preference for real over personal property. An examination of the tax lists for the years 1829 to 1840 shows the preference. Table 4-2 shows the amount of real and personal property held by blacks as recorded by the 1829-1840 tax lists. No assessment of personal property was made between 1830 and 1833.

There were several reasons for this preference for real estate. Buying real estate was a means of increasing one's income; it allowed owners to take in boarders. Ownership of real estate could also increase the chance that one's family might have a decent domicile. One of the larger landholders was Edward Barnes. He did considerable business in Providence and Massachusetts as a real estate speculator and as a landlord. The 1829 tax rolls listed Barnes as having $1,200 worth of real property. In 1865, two years after his death, Barnes's property was auctioned off for $4,812 to pay his creditors. Discounting the probable undervaluation of Barnes's estate, the value of his real property holdings increased 208 percent in a thirty-six-year period, a rate of roughly 2.1 percent per year.[14] Barnes owned three houses on Olney Street and three lots that he was in the process of improving at the time of his death. William J. Brown also appears to have invested in real estate as a means of providing for his family. His will, dated 1881, left a house and lot on Olney Street to his wife, Mary Ann Brown. He also left his wife a share in some other property of which he was part owner, also on Olney Street.[15]

It is hard to make completely accurate estimates about how people spent their money from records that show property holding patterns. Tax, census, and probate records have a greater tendency to show an individual's real property rather than his personal property. Personal property is easier to hide from the tax assessor. It can be divided among a deceased individual's family and friends before the probate authorities can inventory it. Still, bearing these biases in mind, the black, laboring property owners of Providence appear to have been a frugal people. They put their wealth in land to a far greater extent than they put their wealth in personal property. Even the patterns of personal property holding indicate that many of these holdings took the

Table 4-1
NEGROES WHO HELD REAL PROPERTY VALUED AT OVER $500, 1860

NAME	OCCUPATION
Charles Monroe	Gardener
Jacob Hall	Day Laborer
Morris Turner	Whitewasher
John T. Waugh	Waiter
Clarisa Bond	Washerwoman
George Henry	Gardener
John Church	Waiter
George Head	Grocer
John N. Smith	Waiter
Joseph Nahar	Mariner
Antrep Nichols	
John Shumbell	Farmer
John C. Frances	Gardener
Alfred Niger	Barber
Francis Talbot	Porter
Eleanor Eldridge	
Walter Boothe	Laborer
Ichabod Northup	Porter
John W. Addison	Porter
John O. Harzard	Teamer
James M. Cheves	Musketman
Elijah Hall	Butcher
Nathaniel Perkins	Colerer
Manuel Fenner	Horse Farrier
Wm. H. Wilkes	Teamster
Ann Francis (illit.)	
D. W. Gardner	Laborer
Ransom Parker	Laborer
Spencer Waters	Jobber
Samuel Howard	Sexton
James Burke	Saloon keeper

SOURCE: U.S. Census, 1860 (manuscript).

VALUE	NATIVITY	COLOR
$2,000	Massachusetts	Mulatto
$1,000	Maryland	Black
$ 800	Maryland	Black
$1,500	Washington, D.C.	Mulatto
$2,000	Maryland	Black
$3,500	Rhode Island	Mulatto
$1,000	Virginia	Black
$3,000	Rhode Island	Mulatto
$2,000	Maryland	Mulatto
$2,500	Surinam	Mulatto
$ 800	Rhode Island	Black
$2,200	Batvia, East Indies	Mulatto
$2,100	Maryland	Mulatto
$1,900	Rhode Island	Black
$1,100	Rhode Island	Black
$4,800	Rhode Island	Black
$1,500	Maryland	Black
$3,200	Rhode Island	Mulatto
$ 700	Maryland	Black
$2,700	Rhode Island	Mulatto
$3,900	Virginia	Mulatto
$ 700	Massachusetts	Black
$1,000	Rhode Island	Mulatto
$5,000	Rhode Island	Mulatto
$2,000	Rhode Island	Mulatto
$1,200	Rhode Island	Black
$1,200	Rhode Island	Black
$1,800	New Hampshire	Mulatto
$ 800	Maryland	Black
$1,000	Maryland	Black
$ 900	Rhode Island	Black

Table 4-2
VALUE OF PROPERTY HELD BY PROVIDENCE BLACKS,
1829-1860

YEAR	REAL	PERSONAL	REAL AS PERCENTAGE OF ALL PROPERTY
1829	$22,800	$ 1,600	93.4
1834	$18,400	$ 1,200	93.9
1835	$22,800	$ 800	96.5
1836	$22,100	$ 900	96.1
1837	$23,500	$ 1,900	92.5
1838	$29,000	$ 1,200	96.0
1839	$30,400	$ 1,600	95.0
1840	$34,200	$ 1,600	95.5
1860	$61,690	$10,605	85.3

SOURCE: U.S. Census, 1860 (manuscript).

form of investments instead of luxury. Some $3,305 of the personal property owned by members of the community was owned by people who worked with horses, people like veterinarian Manuel Fenner and various teamsters and coachmen. Many of these men doubtless acquired horses and wagons as part of their occupations. George Head's holdings also suggest that a large amount of the personal property in the community may have been occupationally related. He was a grocer; the 1860 census listed him as having $2,000 worth of personal property. It seems likely that the inventory from his grocery store was included in this figure.[16]

Probate records tend to confirm that these wealthiest members of the Providence black community spent relatively little on personal luxuries. Community spokesman and chronicler William J. Brown's personal property inventory reveals a little about his daily life. The 1885 inventory of his property lists the standard furnishings of the times: chairs, beds, kerosene lamps, a wood stove, two rocking chairs, and other ordinary artifacts. A few of his possessions reflected his lifelong religiosity and his interest in reading and writing. One of his possessions was listed as an "old large family bible," perhaps one that had been in his family's possession since their eighteenth-century membership in Providence's First Baptist Church. Also listed in the inventory were "a lot of books" and "an old fashioned writing desk," perhaps the one that he used to compose his autobiography and other writings.[17]

Other estate inventories of those who acquired real property reveal the same pattern of household furnishings and little else. There were some exceptions. Waiter John Waugh owned a piano, and gardener George Henry had a number of gardening tools listed among his possessions. Perhaps the probate records are most remarkable for not showing any of this group as having spent money on a luxury such as a horse and carriage, revealing perhaps the sort of dedication that turned these laborers into property holders.[18]

The literary sources provide some clue as to how this group of manual laborers managed to acquire their property. One of the property holders for whom we have a biography, Eleanor Eldridge, acquired and retained her holdings through a combination of very hard work and white patronage. By 1860, Eldridge, then seventy-five years old, had retired from her life-long work as a laundress. She had been swindled out of $500 in 1839 and had had to post a $500 bond to get her brother released from prison earlier that decade. Despite these difficulties, she had managed to recoup some of these losses because of two biographies sponsored by philanthropic women in Providence.[19]

George Henry's autobiography indicated that he increased his wealth by taking advantage of Providence's racial mores. Specifically looking for tasks that white workers felt were fit only for blacks, Henry roamed the streets of Providence looking for whitewashing and gardening jobs. He also operated a street watering and sweeping service. He met with marked success. The tax rolls for 1850 listed him as having $800 worth of real property; in 1860 his holdings had increased to $3,500 worth of real property.[20]

Although William Brown is not listed among the major property holders, his story is also instructive. He started out as a servant to a white family in his youth. Later he became a mariner; later still he bought out a shoemaking concern that had been owned by Enoc Freeman. By the census of 1860, Brown was listed as a small businessman, and Freeman was a laborer owning some $250 worth of property.[21]

The census of 1860 shows an interesting development among

these more prosperous elements of the Providence black community. Even though they had acquired property by dint of manual labor, they seem to have been preparing their children for more prestigious occupations. George Nahar, the Surinam-born mariner, had a son, Joseph, who was a clerk. Alfred Niger, the successful barber, had two sons who were following the printing trade and another son, Henry, who was a lathe operator. James M. Cheves, the musketman from Virginia, had a son, George, who was a clerk. Even though political activist Ichabod Northup remained an unskilled laborer, his son, Ichabod, Jr., had opened up his own shoemaking business.[22]

Those who were economic successes were also generally people of relatively modest occupational attainment. Why is it that the minister, the teacher, or the doctor did not find their way into this group? Indeed, why is it that such people did not surpass this collection of unskilled and semiskilled workers? Table 4-3 presents a list of black professionals in Providence, as revealed by the 1860 census.

Table 4-3
BLACK PROFESSIONALS IN PROVIDENCE, 1860

NAME	OCCUPATION	NATIVITY
George Pearce	Clerk	Rhode Island
George Nahar	Clerk	Rhode Island
Samuel Flint	Physician	Nova Scotia
Sarah Baxter	Doctress	Massachusetts
Sherman Mars	Engineer	Africa
James Hall	Clergy (Methodist)	Maryland
Joshua Jordan	Clerk	Rhode Island
Lewis L. Lewis	Clergy (Methodist)	Maryland
Deaton Donell	Clergy (Methodist)	Connecticut
Jane M. Allen	Music teacher	New York
Robert Halloway	Engineer	Virginia
William F. Johnson	Lecturer	Maryland
Charles Cozzens	Clerk	Rhode Island
George Cheves	Clerk	Virginia
Joseph W. Greene	Music teacher	Rhode Island
Samuel Rodman	Doctor	Rhode Island
Manuel Fenner	Horse farrier (veterinarian)	Rhode Island

SOURCE: U.S. Census, 1860 (manuscript).

Of this group, only Samuel Rodman and Manuel Fenner were listed as owning any property. Fenner was a highly successful veterinarian who had managed to acquire $5,000 worth of real estate by virtue of his skill at tending horses. Rodman had land valued at $400. Rodman had not always practiced medicine; the census of 1850 lists him as an Indian trader. It is thus unclear whether he was a somewhat successful small businessman who took up medicine to enhance his prestige or a relatively unsuccessful businessman who took up medicine to increase his income.[23]

Fifty-nine percent of the professionals were born outside of Rhode Island. If clerks are not counted, nine of the remaining twelve, or 75 percent, of the professionals were non-Rhode Island natives. Of those who had been born outside of Rhode Island, only Sarah Baxter and Deaton Donnell had appeared in Providence in the census of 1850. Table 4-4 presents a list of professionals who appeared in the 1850 census.

Table 4-4
BLACK PROFESSIONALS IN PROVIDENCE, 1850

NAME	OCCUPATION	NATIVITY
Abraham Bowen	Clerk	Rhode Island
Charles Cozzens	Clerk	Rhode Island
Jeremiah Aster	Clergy (Baptist)	Massachusetts
George Lawrence	Teacher	New York
Deaton Donnell	Clergy (Methodist)	Connecticut
Freeline Williams	Physician	Virginia
Levi Wheaton	Physician	Rhode Island
Joseph Hicks	Clergy (Methodist)	New York
William B. Lemington	Physician	Rhode Island
George Head	Clerk	Rhode Island
Stephen Spiwell	Clerk	Rhode Island
Edward Scon	Clergy (Free will Baptist)	Virginia

SOURCE: U.S. Census, 1850 (manuscript).

Providence seems to have been a difficult place for black professionals. Itinerant black professionals moved into Providence, practiced their professions for a time, and then left.

Men like Asa Goldsbury, one of the first teachers at the African Union Meeting House school, John W. Lewis, minister and temperance leader in the 1830s, and Alexander Crummel, minister and political leader of the late 1830s and early 1840s, all left Providence and pursued their careers elsewhere. Of the professionals found in the 1850 census, only Charles Cozzens, the clerk born in Rhode Island, and Deaton Donnell, the Methodist minister from Connecticut, still practiced their professions in 1860. Because Cozzens had been active in the Whig party, his persistence might be attributed to political connections. It is also interesting to note that George Head, who was a clerk in 1850, became a grocer by 1860. The 1860 census lists him as the owner of $3,000 worth of real and $2,000 worth of personal property. In the 1850 census, 50 percent of the professionals came from out of state. If clerks are not included, the figure rises even higher (seven out of eight, or 87.5 percent).[24]

The nature of the black professional's clientele may explain why professionals did not seem to do very well in Providence, why they rarely acquired property, and why they usually left the city after a short time. Black ministers preached to black congregations, black teachers taught black pupils, black doctors had black patients. The black professional was thus restricted to practicing his profession among one of the poorest segments of Providence's society. On the other hand, the black manual laborer or small businessman, or even a veterinarian like Manuel Fenner, could cultivate a white clientele. Wealthy whites could patronize black barbers or laundresses or gardeners without violating any racial norms—not so with black professionals. This pattern of an almost total lack of property holding among black professionals in Providence may have been peculiar to cities and towns that had relatively small black communities. The large number of Negroes in Philadelphia probably allowed black professionals to do business in a great enough volume to offset partially the fact that their clientele was restricted. This was not the case in Providence's relatively small black community, so the black professional was a transient figure in Providence. While white Providence was somewhat prepared to reward the diligent black servant, it seems to have been prepared to do little for the black professional. The frustration that doubtless contributed to the brief residences of black professionals also contributed to their lack of economic success. Given the itinerant nature of the black professional, it becomes all the more understandable why the black community constantly turned to men like William J. Brown and Ichabod Northup for leadership. While both the professional and the hard-working successful manual laborer represented the highest aspirations of the community, it was the laborers like Northup and Brown who constituted a permanent part of the community. These were the people with the proven records of leadership who were called on time and time again as the black community sought to better itself.

The census of 1860 also furnishes other information. We see blacks and whites living in the same households, despite the prejudices of the day. Masters and servants are among these, as would be expected, but there are others. There were seven interracial marriages, despite Rhode Island's prohibition of such. One mixed couple was from Argentina—Raimund Valle, a white Argentinian who listed his occupation as "gentlemen," and his black Argentine wife, Nigacia. Another mixed marriage was that of Abraham Bicknell, a black drayman who lived with his white wife, Lavina. The city's registrar's report indicates that an illegal marriage between a white sailor and a black woman had taken place in 1860. In addition to these cases, several white workingmen lived in houses inhabited by blacks. Their occupations and lack of property suggest that they were cohabiters rather than employers; some were probably boarders or renting rooms from black home owners.

These cases raise several questions. We know that Providence was the scene of conflict between blacks and white workingmen, yet in Providence and indeed in many other northeastern cities, the white and black poor and working classes often lived side by side. What was daily interaction like between these two groups? A riot like the Hardscrabble one or the New York draft riot and major political conflicts like the Dorr war reflect the conflict that existed. But the anonymous white sailor and his black wife, noted by Edward Snow, Providence's city registrar, or Charles Monroe, a mulatto gardener from Massachusetts who lived with his white wife, Sarah, and was the landlord to another mixed couple, Richard Howard, a white gardener from Connecticut and his mulatto wife, Sarah—all give us a different picture of race relations.

One of the areas that students of race relations still need to explore is the pattern of day-to-day relations between blacks and working-class whites. It is likely that while members of these two groups confronted each other during times of high political and social tension, they also coexisted relatively peaceably, perhaps even amicably, on an everyday basis. Brown, for example, noted that during the height of his Whig activity, some of his best customers were Democrats, presumably white workingmen. This might be an especially crucial problem to examine for those interested in the conflicts between blacks and immigrants. Immigrants did not come to the United States with anti-black prejudice; they learned it here. Often immigrants initially settled in neighborhoods that had large numbers of blacks, attracted by relatively cheap rents. In Boston, the majority of white women married to black men were immigrants.[25]

Clearly the census reveals that some broke through the barriers of hostility that existed between black and white. It is interesting to note that the two white men in Providence who married black women worked in professions that blacks worked in, in large numbers. Although this indicates that perhaps there were somewhat different attitudes on the part of whites who had black co-workers, clearly these are too few cases to do anything more than suggest hypotheses. We still need to know much more about relations between blacks and working-class whites in times other than the periods of high conflict with which we are more familiar.

The censuses of 1850 and 1860 enable us to take a closer look at the occupational structure of the Providence Negro community.[26] For this purpose, occupations have been divided into four categories: unskilled, artisan, entrepreneur, and professional. The unskilled category includes laborers, washerwomen, hack drivers, whitewashers, porters, laundresses, painters, sextons, servants, waiters, gardeners, and cooks. Included among the artisans are mariners, seamstresses, upholsterers, farmers, printers, lathe operators, watch repairmen, blacksmiths, tailors, and bakers. The entrepreneurs consist of barbers, shoemakers, and grocers. Clerks, doctors, veterinarians, engineers, and teachers are numbered

among the professionals. There is an ambiguity in these classifica-
tions. The distinction between the unskilled and the professional
classes is reasonably clear, but the artisan and entrepreneurial
categories tend to overlap. Barbers, shoemakers, and grocers were
included among the entrepreneurs because the literary evidence
suggests that people in those occupations tended to operate independent enterprises; those listed in the artisan category tended
to be employees. Still, there is an inherent ambiguity between the
two categories, and it could be convincingly argued that perhaps
they should be lumped together. Also, a word or two about the
professional category is in order, many of the individuals and occupations listed in the professional category would not have been
placed in that category if this had been a study of a white community. The reason for the inclusion of some occupations with
slight claim to professional status is the limited occupational opportunities that the Negro community had available. Occupations that were included in the professional category were those
that seemed to depend to some degree on formal education, even
if only on the elementary literacy and ciphering level. Thus clerks
are included because their jobs required a basic education—the
ability to read, write, and do arithmetic. The other professionals
probably had had an elementary school education, supplemented
by their own studies of theology, medicine, and other subjects.
In a community most of whose members labored at tasks that
would not have required any formal education, these people were
an occupational elite, which is why they have been labeled professionals.

The overwhelming majority of Negro workers were concentrated in the unskilled occupations; few were fortunate enough
to escape the larger society's determination that Negroes should
be relegated to those tasks that white men and women did not
want to perform. (See tables 4-5 and 4-6.) Yet the community
was not homogeneous. Among the working people of the community, there were blacks and mulattoes, those born in Rhode
Island and those who came from elsewhere, and, of course, men
and women. In 1860, some 80 percent of the workers in the community were black; 20 percent were mulattoes. (See tables 4-7
and 4-8.) Men comprised 63 percent of the labor force; women
accounted for 37 percent. The number of working women had

risen dramatically between 1850 and 1860. Women were only 2 percent of the community's work force in 1850. It appears that the depression of 1857 had driven large numbers out of their households in search of employment to help sustain themselves and their families. Forty-four percent of the work force was born in Rhode Island, 57 percent elsewhere.

Table 4-5
OCCUPATIONS OF NEGROES, 1850

TYPE OF OCCUPATION	NUMBER	PERCENTAGE OF WORK FORCE
Unskilled	212	67.3
Artisan	49	15.6
Entrepreneur	41	13.0
Professional	13	4.1
No occupation listed	69	Missing
Total	384	100.0

SOURCE: U.S. Census, 1850 (manuscript).

Table 4-6
OCCUPATIONS OF NEGROES, 1860

TYPE OF OCCUPATION	NUMBER	PERCENTAGE OF WORK FORCE
Unskilled	415	75.0
Artisan	72	13.0
Entrepreneur	51	9.2
Professional	15	2.7

SOURCE: U.S. Census, 1860 (manuscript).

Table 4-7
OCCUPATIONS OF NEGROES, BY COLOR, 1860

TYPE OF OCCUPATION	BLACKS		MULATTOES	
	Number	Percentage	Number	Percentage
Unskilled	341	77.3	74	66.1
Artisan	55	12.5	17	15.2
Entrepreneur	36	8.2	15	13.4
Professional	9	2.0	6	5.4

SOURCE: U.S. Census, 1860 (manuscript).

Table 4-8
OCCUPATIONS OF NEGROES, BY COLOR, 1850

TYPE OF OCCUPATION	BLACKS		MULATTOES	
	Number	Percentage	Number	Percentage
Unskilled	153	70.2	59	60.8
Artisan	32	14.7	17	17.5
Entrepreneur	23	10.6	18	18.6
Professional	10	4.5	3	3.1
Total	218	69.2	97	30.79

SOURCE: U.S. Census, 1850 (manuscript).

There were differences in the occupational levels attained by
various segments of the community. Some of these differences
were doubtless accidental; some indicate that accidents of birth
helped some elements of the community attain greater success
than others in climbing the occupational pyramid. Other variations are hard to draw any inferences from; there are too few
cases. One of the differences that was significant was sex. Men
had few opportunities, women even fewer. Nineteenth-century
sexual mores still managed to make life more difficult for the
working woman than the workingman, even in a community
where securing a livelihood could be very hard. The men of the
community were much more successful than the women in get-
ting work other than unskilled labor. In 1860 over 30 percent
of the men were in occupations above the unskilled level. That
same year, only about 16 percent of the women worked in occupations above the unskilled levels. (See tables 4-6, 4-9, 4-11.)[27]

The meager occupational opportunities open to female workers helps explain a nearly 8 percent increase (from a little over
67 percent to 75 percent) in the percentage of workers in the unskilled category between 1850 and 1860. The women who
entered the work force in the intervening decade depressed the
overall occupational level of the community. The downturn in
male occupational level was less severe than the figures for the
community as a whole. In 1850, a little over 66 percent of the
men worked at unskilled occupations; that figure rose to over
69 percent in 1860. Still, these figures probably understate the
true importance of working women to the economic life of

Providence's Negroes. The 1850 census's listing of eight women as having occupations would not have accounted for significant numbers of housewives who supplemented family income by taking in other people's laundry, caring for other families' children, or occasionally cooking meals for other families. These kinds of casual, irregular jobs were no doubt missed by the census marshal, yet they would have constituted a significant, though to us largely hidden, part of the community's occupational structure. (See tables 4-5, 4-6, 4-9, 4-10, 4-11, and 4-13.)

Table 4-9
OCCUPATIONS OF NEGRO MEN, 1860

TYPE OF OCCUPATION	NUMBER	PERCENTAGE OF WORK FORCE
Unskilled	243	69.6
Artisan	47	13.5
Entrepreneur	46	13.2
Professional	13	3.7
Total	349	100.0

SOURCE: U.S. Census, 1860 (manuscript).

Table 4-10
OCCUPATIONS OF NEGRO MEN, 1850

TYPE OF OCCUPATION	NUMBER	PERCENTAGE OF WORK FORCE
Unskilled	204	66.4
Artisan	49	16.8
Entrepreneur	41	13.4
Professional	13	4.2

SOURCE: U. S. Census, 1850 (manuscript).

The community consisted of more than men and women. There were color differences as well. The role of the mulatto in northern Afro-American communities is relatively difficult to assess. In South Africa, mulattoes are treated as a race separate from blacks by law. In Brazil and other parts of Latin America, strong cultural and social practices have institutionalized distinctions between blacks and mulattoes. In the United States, the distinctions have been less precise. Afro- and Euro-Americans

Table 4-11
OCCUPATIONS OF NEGRO WOMEN, 1860

TYPE OF OCCUPATION	NUMBERS	PERCENTAGE OF WORK FORCE
Unskilled	172	84.3
Artisan	25	12.3
Entrepreneur	5	2.5
Professional	2	1.0
No occupation listed 3	3	Missing
Total 207		100.0

SOURCE: U.S. Census, 1860 (manuscript).

have certainly distinguished between the two groups. In the
nineteenth century, some even used a classification scheme that
approached the lexicographical rigor of those employed in Latin
America; people were designated as mulattoes, quadroons, and
octoroons. Southern mulattoes often enjoyed more privileges
as slaves and freedmen than their black counterparts. Still, these
distinctions occurred within a context that treated all Negroes
as part of a group, a group whose rights and privileges were different from and inferior to those of whites. Color prejudice and
family ties might have allowed mulattoes to rise in dispropor-
tionate numbers to the top of Negro society, but they did not
permit escape from the group. Only, arguably, in Louisiana did
mulattoes escape the castelike confinement that Negroes were
subject to, allowing them to form a separate and distinct group.
The peculiar situation of Louisiana mulattoes was largely due to
that state's Spanish and French cultural heritage.

For the rest of the United States, however, and especially in
the North, the distinctions made between blacks and mulattoes
were largely informal, not institutional. These informal distinctions could make differences in individual lives. They affected
choice of marriage partners and the willingness of whites to extend those opportunities that society permitted Negroes; at times,
they even determined social status within some Negro communities.

Mulattoes did better than blacks in the occupational pyramid
to which Providence Negroes were restricted. Of the 112 mulatto workers listed in the 1860 census, 38 (34 percent) worked at

Table 4-12
OCCUPATIONS OF BLACKS, 1860

TYPE OF OCCUPATION	NUMBER	PERCENTAGE OF WORK FORCE
Unskilled	341	77.3
Artisan	55	12.5
Entrepreneur	36	8.2
Professional	9	2
No occupation listed	2	Missing
Total	443	100.0

SOURCE: U.S. Census, 1860 (manuscript).

Table 4-13
OCCUPATIONS OF MULATTOES, 1860

TYPE OF OCCUPATION	NUMBER	PERCENTAGE OF WORK FORCE
Unskilled	74	66.1
Artisan	17	15.2
Entrepreneur	15	13.4
Professional	6	5.4
No occupation listed	1	Missing
Total	113	100.0

SOURCE: U. S. Census, 1860 (manuscript).

jobs above the unskilled level. Blacks did not fare as well. Only 29 percent, or 100 of the 341, were above the lowest rungs of the community's occupational ladder. The 1850 census reveals similar disparities between the two groups. That year, 65 (30 percent) black workers were above the unskilled level, while 39 percent, or 38 of the 97 mulatto workers, were artisans, entrepreneurs, or professionals. There were differences in the occupational patterns of the two groups, though the differences were not great enough for us to conclude that mulattoes had significantly greater occupational opportunities than blacks. (See table 4-7 and 4-8.)[28]

Success in climbing the occupational ladder was not necessarily synonymous with success in accumulating wealth for Providence's Negroes. Were mulattoes generally more successful

than blacks in acquiring wealth? Table 4-1 shows that of the
thirty-one major property holders, sixteen were blacks and
fifteen were mulattoes. Mulattoes were about 20 percent of the
labor force, yet they constituted nearly half of the major property holders. In terms of accumulating wealth, mulattoes were
doing significantly better than blacks.[29]

Mulattoes did better than blacks both in attaining the better
occupations and in acquiring wealth. The informal differentia-
tions made by Providence and the rest of American society made
a difference in the opportunities available to the two segments
of the community. Yet, before too much is made of this, a
number of caveats are in order. First, if findings from research
done on Philadelphia prove reliable for other northern cities,
our very ability to distinguish blacks from mulattoes in the census may be suspect. These designations were based on the judgments of census marshals, with differing degrees of accuracy.
And beyond the question of dubious designations, there remains
the fact that while mulattoes were disproportionately represented
in the upper strata of those economic opportunities available to
Providence Negroes, they were not there exclusively. The majority of workers above the unskilled category were black. Half of
the major property owners were black. There were no black jobs
or mulatto jobs; there was a range of occupations open to Negroes,
and mulattoes had somewhat greater access to the better ones.
The overwhelming majority of both groups were in the city's less
desirable jobs and owned no significant amounts of property.
Both were, with few exceptions, hard-working manual laborers
who struggled to maintain an often precarious livelihood. The
different experiences of the two groups should not serve to obscure their far greater similarities.[30]

Sex and color influenced a person's chances for economic
well-being, but these were not the only differences that could
be observed in the community. Just as many left the community
in search of a better life, many came to Providence with a similar
quest. (See table 4-14 through table 4-18.) Many reasons could
have brought a Negro to antebellum Providence. Despite per-
sistent discrimination, Providence was probably the best city,
in one of the better states, in the best region for a free Afro-
American to live. To a free Negro from the South, the ability to

Table 4-14
OCCUPATIONS AND PLACES OF ORIGIN OF PROVIDENCE NEGROES, 1860

TYPE OF OCCUPATION	RHODE ISLAND		MIDDLE ATLANTIC		UPPER SOUTH		TOTAL	
	Number	Percent	Number	Percent	Number	Percent	Number	Percent
Unskilled	183	75.3	50	68.5	122	80.3	415	75.0
Artisan	24	9.9	17	23.3	20	13.2	72	13.0
Entrepreneur	29	11.9	5	6.8	7	4.6	51	9.2
Professional	7	2.9	1	1.4	3	2.0	15	2.7
Number from Region/Percentage of total	243	43.9	73	13.2	152	27.5	553	100.0

TYPE OF OCCUPATION	OTHER SOUTH		NEW ENGLAND		FOREIGN	
	Number	Percent	Number	Percent	Number	Percent
Unskilled	4	66.7	55	75.3	1	16.7
Artisan	2	33.8	6	8.2	3	50.0
Entrepreneur	0	0.0	9	12.3	1	16.7
Professional	0	0.0	3	4.1	1	16.7
Number from Region/Percentage of total		1.1	73	13.2	6	1.1

SOURCE: U.S. Census, 1860 (manuscript).
NOTE: Raw chi - square = 34.39238, with 15 degrees of freedom. Significance = 0.000.

Table 4-15
OCCUPATIONS OF PROVIDENCE BLACKS FROM
THE UPPER SOUTH, 1850

TYPE OF OCCUPATION	NUMBER	PERCENTAGE OF WORK FORCE
Unskilled	39	79.6
Artisan	7	14.3
Entrepreneur	2	4.1
Professional	1	2.0
No occupation listed	10	Missing
Total	59	100.0

SOURCE: U. S. Census, 1850 (manuscript).

Table 4-16
OCCUPATIONS OF PROVIDENCE BLACKS FROM
THE UPPER SOUTH, 1860

TYPE OF OCCUPATION	NUMBER	PERCENTAGE OF WORK FORCE
Unskilled	104	83.9
Artisan	15	12.1
Entrepreneur	3	2.4
Professional	2	1.6
Total	124	100.0

SOURCE: U. S. Census, 1860 (manuscript).

Table 4-17
OCCUPATIONS OF PROVIDENCE MULATTOES
FROM THE UPPER SOUTH, 1850

TYPE OF OCCUPATION	NUMBER	PERCENTAGE OF WORK FORCE
Unskilled	15	71.4
Artisan	3	14.3
Entrepreneur	2	9.5
Professional	1	4.8
No occupation listed	1	Missing
Total	22	100.0

SOURCE: U. S. Census, 1850 (manuscript).

Table 4-18
OCCUPATIONS OF PROVIDENCE MULATTOES
FROM THE UPPER SOUTH, 1860

TYPE OF OCCUPATION	NUMBER	PERCENTAGE OF WORK FORCE
Unskilled	18	64.3
Artisan	5	17.9
Entrepreneur	4	14.3
Professional	1	3.6
Total	28	100.0

SOURCE: U. S. Census, 1860 (manuscript).

live in a place where he would not constantly have to show his manumission papers to any white man who demanded them could add a new dimension to his freedom. To a fugitive slave, Providence might offer a haven if he could hide from the slave catchers. A man from Connecticut might be attracted by the political rights this neighboring state extended to him, a recognition of his citizenship denied him in his native state. Another person, perhaps from New Hampshire, might want the association and comfort that a Negro community would provide. A mariner whose ship put in at Providence might decide that the city was as good a place as any other in which to put down roots. Others might be part of that mobile mass of free Afro-Americans in the North constantly searching for, and all too often not finding, a place where their talents and energies would meet with decent financial reward.

Whatever brought the individual to Providence, a substantial number, 57 percent, of the work force in the community was born outside the state. The results for those from out of state vary. Afro-Yankees from other parts of New England had an occupational distribution that closely paralleled that of native Rhode Islanders. Those from the middle Atlantic states were doing slightly better than natives, those from the upper South somewhat worse. One group did significantly better than any other in terms of the sorts of jobs that they were able to secure: the foreign born. Of the six foreign-born workers, five were above the unskilled level and two were major property holders. There are too few of these individuals to attempt to ascribe any statistical significance to their success, yet they are an interesting enough group to warrant a brief examination. The six were: Joseph Nahar, a mariner born in Surinam, who owned $2,500 worth of real estate; Edwin Wilson, a laborer born in Cuba; John H. Shumbell, a farmer born in Batvia, the East Indies, who owned $2,200 worth of real estate; Sherman Mars, an engineer from Africa; and Edwin J. Lems, a barber born in Bermu The sixth, Thomas Winslow from Ireland, was perhaps the most unusual. He worked in an industrial occupation as a machinist, indicating that, at least in terms of his occupation, he more closely followed the patterns prevailing among Irish immigrants Whether the relative prosperity of the handful of foreign immigrants was accidental or an indication that some self-selectior process brought these black immigrants to antebellum Providence cannot be determined here. It may be that a black person who would immigrate to antebellum America would have to have unusual circumstances and skills to come to a land known for slavery and severe discrimination. In any event the life of the foreign Negro immigrant in antebellum America merits further investigation. (See table 4-14.)

Conclusion

Censuses, tax directories, and similar sources can tell us much. They help fill in the gaps in the world revealed by men like Brown, Henry, Northup, and the other blacks and whites who concerned themselves with the fortunes of the Providence black community. While those people concerned themselves with the many tribulations and some triumphs of the stable, working-class black men and women who waged a constant struggle for equality in the land of their birth, they rarely indulged in sociological speculations about their community. They did not have the time. But government agencies, imperfectly no doubt, did collect the sort of raw data that permit us to contrast different elements of the black community and the black community with the white people of Providence. Such material cannot be a substitute for the insider's perceptions of a Brown or even the observations of a sympathetic outsider like McDougall. Literary sources supply us with the hundreds of intimate details of the life of a community that we would never have otherwise seen. Nonetheless, without the kinds of social and economic information supplied by statistical sources, we would have missed an important dimension of black life in antebellum Providence, a dimension that reveals much about the social structure of the community. Our knowledge of that social structure helps us to understand why extraordinary men with very ordinary jobs led the community.

Notes

1. *Census of Providence* (Providence, 1855), pp. 5-16; Edwin M. Snow, *Census of Rhode Island, 1865* (Providence: Providence Press, 1867), pp. xliv, xlv; Peter J. Coleman, *The Transformation of Rhode Island*, p. 62; *U.S. Censuses*, 1850 and 1860 (manuscripts).

2. Snow, *Census, 1865*, pp. 5-16.

3. *Census of Providence.*

4. *U.S. Censuses, 1850 and 1860* (published). This sexual imbalance was also the pattern among blacks in Philadelphia. See Theodore Hershberg and Henry Williams, "Mulattoes and Blacks: Intra-group Color Differences and Social Stratification in Nineteenth Century Philadelphia," in *Philadelphia: Work, Space, Family and Group Experience in the 19th Century*, ed. Theodore Hershberg (New York: Oxford, 1981), pp. 402-3.

5. Ibid. By way of comparison, the percentage of female-headed households among blacks in 1978 was a little over 39 percent. See *The Social and Economic Status of the Black Population in the United States, An Historical View, 1790-1978* (Washington, D.C.: Department of Commerce, n.d.), p. 175.

6. Snow, *Census*, p. lxxviii; U.S. Census, 1860 (manuscript).

7. Ibid.; x^2 = 84.5 $p < 0.001$.

8. U.S. Censuses, 1850 and 1860 (manuscript).

9. Ibid.

10. Blacks were not among those listed in the following occupations found in the *Census of Providence* (1855): contractors, card markers, combmakers, clothing dealers, coal dealers, cotton waste dealers, copper smiths, corset makers, cigar store keepers, confectioners, caulkers, cotton dealers, carpet dealers, crockery dealers, carvers, carpet weavers, dry-good dealers, druggists, die sinkers, dentists, designers, dredgers, draughtsmen, distillers, dye stuff dealers, dipper makers, dye wood cutters, engine turners, engravers, editors, expressmen, factory operatives, railroad firemen, furniture dealers, fish dealers, file makers, fancy goods dealers, gas inspectors, gas fitters, glue makers, grain dealers, gilders, harness makers, hotel keepers, hatters, hardware dealers, hose makers, iron dealers, iron founders, iron fence makers, image makers, junk dealers, japanners, lumber dealers, lamp makers, leather dealers, leather dressers, lamplighter looking glass makers, lapidaries, lawyers, librarians, manufacturers, merchants, molders, millwrights, milkmen, marketmen, machine printers, music dealers, marble workers, millers, movers of buildings, nail makers, nutmakers, oystermen, overseers, oil dealers, organ builders, policemen, plumbers, pattern makers, paint and oil dealers, planary workers, printers platers, paper makers, plane makers, pain killer makers, paper hangers, plough makers, pianoforte dealers, picture frame makers, press men, paper box dealers, polishers, pilots, professors, phrenologists, planters, picker makers, reed makers, roller covers, rolling mill workers, riggers, razor grinders, rope makers, refiners, rag gatherers, surveyors, spice mill owners, slaters, superintendents, stucco workers, stair builders, sash and blind makers, shoe dealers, saloon keepers, safe makers, silversmiths, soapmakers, stove dealers, stable keepers, stove mounters, shoe binders,

sausage makers, spile drivers, sail makers, sheet iron workers, shipping officers, spar makers, sculptors, trunkmakers, tinmen, tarpers, tobacconists, tanners and curriers, tool makers, treasurers, tube makers, ticket masters, telegraph operators, undertakers, varnishers, variety store keepers, weavers, weighers, watchmen, wire makers, wooden ware dealers, wool sorters, and wool dealers.

11. Other studies of Negroes in northern cities indicate that the exclusion of black workers from factories may have been a pattern that persisted in the North until World War I. Herbert Gutman in *The Black Family in Slavery and Freedom, 1750-1925* (New York: Vintage, 1976), p. xviii, reports that a study he and Laurence A. Glasco conducted of blacks in Buffalo, New York, indicated that there were few black factory workers in that city until the 1920s. David Katzman's study, *Before the Ghetto: Black Detroit in the Nineteenth Century* (Urbana: University of Illinois Press, 1973), p. 105, also indicates that blacks were underrepresented among Detroit's factory workers. In his pioneering study of blacks in a northern city, *The Philadelphia Negro*, W. E. B. Du Bois attributed the absence of blacks in large manufacturing concerns to racial discrimination. See W. E. B. Du Bois, *The Philadelphia Negro* (New York: Schocken Books, 1967), p. 123.

12. *Census of Providence* (1855); U.S. Census, 1860 (manuscript). If we measure the actual number of black industrial workers ($N = 7$) and compare this with what we would have expected if race and membership in the industrial work force were unrelated ($N = 91$), we see that it is highly improbable that being black and being absent from industrial occupations were unrelated. $x^2 = 77.5\ p < 0.001$

13. *Providence Town-Tax Records, 1829-1840* (Printed by Hutchens and Weeden); U.S. Census, 1860 (manuscript). Growth rates and overall increases have been adjusted to take into account a 3 percent deflationary difference between the 1829 dollar and the 1860 dollar as measured by the wholesale price index. See Lance E. Davis et al., *American Economic Growth, An Economist's History of the United States* (New York: Harper and Row, 1972), p. 364.

14. *Providence Town-Tax Records;* U.S. Census, 1860 (manuscript).

15. Ibid.; Providence Probate Records: The Estates of Edward Barnes and William J. Brown (manuscripts). Rates of growth and percentage increase adjusted for 93 percent inflation rate as measured by wholesale price index. This jump in the inflation rate can largely be attributed to the Civil War. See Davis et al., *American Economic Growth*, pp. 364-65.

16. U.S. Census, 1860 (manuscript).

17. Providence Probate Records: Estate of William J. Brown.

18. Providence Probate Records: Estates of John Waugh and George Henry (manuscripts).

19. Frances McDougall, *Memoirs of Eleanor Eldridge* and *Eleanor's Second Book*.

20. George Henry, *The Life of George Henry*.

21. William J. Brown, *The Life of William J. Brown*; U.S. Census, 1860 (manuscript).

22. U.S. Census, 1860 (manuscript).

23. U.S. Census, 1850 (manuscript).

24. Ibid.; U.S. Census 1860 (manuscript).

25. James Oliver Horton and Lois E. Horton, *Black Bostonians*, pp. 21-2

26. In this section the term *Negro* will be used for the whole Negro community. The terms *black* and *mulatto* will be used for different elements of the community.

27. $x^2 = 7.08\ p < 0.01$.

28. For 1850 data, $x^2 = 1.1\ p < 0.50$; for 1860 data, $x^2 = 3.57\ p < 0.1$

29. $x^2 = 13.5\ p < 0.001$.

30. Hershberg and Williams found that 47 percent of those listed as mulattoes in the federal census of 1850 for Philadelphia, were listed as blacks a decade later. Hershberg and Williams, "Mulattoes and Blacks," p. 397.

PROVIDENCE, MODERNIZATION, AND THE EMERGENCE OF NORTHERN RACISM

5

On January 3, 1859, a one-hundred-year-old man, James How-land, died in Jamestown, Rhode Island. He was the last slave in that state. His life and death had a chronological significance, for while he never made the transition from slave to freedman, his lifetime spanned the slave era and the emancipation of Rhode Island blacks. A great deal of change occurred during Howland's lifetime, though it is likely that as a slave living on the island of Jamestown, he was only peripherally, if at all, a participant in the social metamorphoses that occurred in Rhode Island race relations. Still, Howland's life presents a series of historical benchmarks against which black life in Rhode Island can be measured.[1]

During his childhood most Rhode Island blacks were slaves. Some labored on the Narragansett plantations; others lived and worked in towns and cities like Newport, Bristol, and Providence. In Howland's youth, the Revolutionary period, blacks started gaining freedom in greater numbers. Some enlisted with the Revolutionary forces; more were freed with the end of the Revolution. By the beginning of the nineteenth century, while Howland was still relatively young, most Rhode Island blacks were free. While Howland was middle-aged, blacks in Providence began developing social institutions, which nurtured black leadership.

As age overtook Howland, black men in Providence and other parts of Rhode Island began to participate in the political process.

Howland was eighty-three at the time of the Dorr war, eighty-
nine when the black voters of Providence decided that their
party loyalties overrode their dissatisfaction with Whig candidate Zachary Taylor. During Howland's ninety-eighth year,
Dowling, Northup, and the others made their unsuccessful attempt to integrate the Rhode Island school system. His death
was on the eve of the Civil War.

During Howland's life, race relations in Rhode Island took
several turns. In his youth, blacks were slaves, and many whites
lived lives that were little better than those of slaves. These
laboring peoples were looked down upon by society generally,
and there is every indication that relations between the white
poor and black slaves were rather good. After the Revolution,
there was a period when the law in Rhode Island made few
formal distinctions between black and white. The nineteenth
century brought new divisions between the races, especially
between working-class whites and blacks. Toward the end of
Howland's life, blacks in Rhode Island had made some progress
in breaching the caste wall that had been erected around them;
they had developed leaders and organizations that expressed
their hopes for better lives. Alliances had formed between black
and some whites, mostly middle- and upper-class whites. Some
rights had been won, yet much remained to be done.

If Howland's life can serve as a series of benchmarks that
remind us of the evolution of race relations in Providence, it
can also help remind us of developments elsewhere in the nation. These developments can help explain and put into context the story of race relations in Providence and other northern cities. Howland's lifetime encompassed the eras of the birth
of the American nation and the growth of institutions and
practices that in many ways still shape modern America. Before Howland's death, the present boundaries of the continental
United States were established. Well before Howland had reached
his last decade, most states had rejected a property-based suffrage in favor of legislation that allowed rich and poor to go to
the polls. This democratic spirit did not extend to women, and
it extended to black men in only a handful of states; nonetheless, the idea of mass-based political participation was established
early in nineteenth-century America, in Howland's lifetime. In

Howland's childhood, the agricultural and commercial nature of the Rhode Island and national economies was readily apparent. The twin foundations of the colonial economies were the crops produced in coastal farms and the ships that exchanged these crops for the riches of other colonies and nations. By the time Howland was an adult, a vigorous industrial economy was overtaking the commercial economy that had dominated so much of eighteenth-century life. The textile mill and the iron foundry, aided by new railroads, canals, and steam-propelled vehicles that traversed water and railway, were transforming life throughout America, particularly in urban areas like Providence. New populations came to cities; new forms of social and political organizations emerged. In short, in one man's lifetime, a nation underwent that multifaceted process of upheaval called modernization.

Those nineteenth-century developments that helped to shape modern American society during the course of Howland's lifetime had different effects on black and white Americans. Many of the changes that generally contributed to the economic and social growth of the country also helped to sharpen the distinctions between black and white in American society. The circumstances and institutions that expanded the horizons and opportunities of many white Americans in the nineteenth century were frequently in those sectors of society least likely to include blacks. The very geographic expansion of the nation illustrates this point. It is not necessary to delve into the many critiques and defenses of Frederick Jackson Turner's *The Frontier in American History* to acknowledge that for many white Americans, the western lands that were added to the United States represented tremendous opportunities. Yeoman farmer, rancher, cotton planter, trader, miner, and merchant all found that the new lands offered increased possibilities for wealth for both the individual and his family. If Turner's assertion that the frontier was a safety valve or that American democracy was a product of the West now seems somewhat overblown, it nonetheless seems clear that large numbers of ordinary Americans were able to move westward in search of better lives, in the hopes that the abundant lands and resources of the West could be put to their advantage.[2]

Black and white did not have equal access to the opportunities that the new states and territories offered. Many of the western states passed laws explicitly prohibiting black settlement. Those western states that did permit black migration did not grant blacks even the semblance of equal rights occasionally found in some of the northeastern states. Turner's frontier democracy thesis is in fact directly reversed when viewed in racial terms. While blacks could legally vote in New York, Rhode Island, Massachusetts, Vermont, New Hampshire, and Maine in the antebellum period, none of the western states permitted black suffrage until after the Civil War.[3]

The older states, where free black populations had developed in the seventeenth and eighteenth centuries, were the ones most comfortable with a free black presence. Free Negroes had differing degrees of rights and privileges in the East. In most of New England, there were few recognized legal differences between free blacks and the white population. In some of the southeastern states, free Negroes could remain in a state and maintain their freedom only by having manumission papers and white sponsors. Yet the sheer numbers of free Negroes in the southeastern states, the results of seventeenth- and eighteenth-century manumissions, caused whites in those states to realize that free blacks were a part, even if an unwelcome part, of their state's population.

The West was different. Largely untouched by Euro and Afro-American settlement in the seventeenth and eighteenth centuries, the western states did not have to come to grips with a previously established free black population. Forces that wished to exclude free blacks from the West could do so, unencumbered by an existing black population. Nor did the western states have a lingering residue of that racially liberal spirit of the late eighteenth century that permitted a measure of de jure equality for blacks in some of the northeastern states. The West was largely a tabula rasa, a clean canvas on which the racially restrictive ideas of early nineteenth-century America could be firmly etched.

One of the few western states that was an exception to this pattern of hostility toward the free Negro was Louisiana. For the free blacks, and more especially the free mulattoes, of that state, the degree of personal liberty and equality that they en-

joyed was actually higher than that accorded their counterparts in the southeastern states. This was because of patterns
of race relations that had developed during the French and
Spanish rule of Louisiana in the eighteenth century. The often
not inconsiderable efforts of nineteenth-century Anglo-American
settlers to curtail the rights that free Negroes had enjoyed in
French and Spanish Louisiana were not entirely successful; sur-
vivals of these rights persisted throughout the antebellum period.
Still, Louisiana was an exception among western states, particularly those of the old Southwest. The very circumstances of its
exceptionalism forcefully reiterate the view that those states
where free Negroes had some measure of acceptance were those
states where free Negroes had been an established part of a state's
population before the nineteenth century.[4]

The free Negro's restrictions in antebellum western settlements
were typical of the relationships between blacks and many of the
changes that were part of the evolution of modern America. For
those concerned with the origins and persistence of racial conflict in northeastern cities like Providence, two of the most important of these changes were the growth of the industrial economy and the expansion of political rights. Ironically, though the
free Negroes of the North were largely bypassed by the burgeoning industrial economy, the factory nonetheless exerted a tremendous influence on the social and economic development of
black populations in northern cities. The factory contributed to,
indeed enhanced, the economic and social marginalization of
blacks in nineteenth-century America. Instead of finding employment in the newer industrial sector of the economy, blacks
were generally relegated to older occupations—those that their
parents and grandparents had performed as slaves in the eighteenth century. The laborer who went to the docks to unload
cargo, the gardener who pulled weeds and raised flowers, the
laundress who daily exchanged baskets of clean clothes for dirty
ones: all were performing tasks in the early and mid-nineteenth
century that their parents and grandparents would have found
quite familiar. In cities like Providence, freedom, even significant
progress in political rights, brought little change in the kinds of
work that most black people were allowed to do.

This exclusion from the increasingly important industrial sector of the economy meant exclusion from many of the dynamic forces that were shaping nineteenth-century American society. The development of industry increased the degree to which the labor force would be stratified by levels of skill. To traditional distinctions between artisans and unskilled laborers would be added new distinctions based on an individual's ability to work with, repair, or adapt the new machinery that was to become a part of the working lives of many nineteenth-century Americans. Black workers did not share in the acquisition of these new skills. In cities like Providence, the black worker was in the curious position of being in a society that increasingly valued literacy and technical skills and yet finding that education or technical skill played little role in enhancing his economic well-being. The major property holders (see table 4-1) among Providence Negroes were not those who had the skills or education that in some way related to the newer forms of economic activity. Instead for the most part, the good or bad fortunes of black workers seem to have depended on their ability to maintain good personal relations with white employers.

Exclusion from the factory had important economic and occupational effects, but it may have had even more important social consequences. While white workers were moving away from that premodern master-servant relationship that was the common experience of the black and white poor in the eighteenth century and toward a modern employer-employee relationship with the upper classes, blacks in many ways were less able to do so. Blacks were no longer in the old eighteenth-century master-slave relationship, to be sure. By the middle of the nineteenth century, most blacks lived in their own households, attended black churches, and were members and officers of their own organizations. Still, the kinds of employment opportunities open to most blacks kept them in a close, dependent relationship with wealthier whites. This was at a time when working-class whites were forming the sorts of class-oriented organizations that reflected the economic and social dynamics of an increasingly modern, industrial society. The different experiences of black and white laboring people partly explain why white workers organized their movements for political, economic, and social betterment along class lines, while blacks organized across class lines, usually addressing their appeals to the more aristocratic elements of the white community.

The different patterns of black and white employment also influenced the way upper-class whites viewed blacks on the one hand and white workers on the other. A wealthy white employer might develop a strong personal, paternalistic relationship with his black coachman or maid and yet might deal with his factory hands on a highly impersonal basis. This might be especially true if the coachman's family had served the employer's family for generations back to the eighteenth-century era of master and slave. The kind of worker in the factory might also significantly affect how that employer perceived the laborers of the two races. When the daughters of rural Yankees came to New England factories, hoping to earn enough money to help future husbands buy farms, the level of personal concern and paternalistic interest was high. When the often-despised Irish immigrants became the hands that made the factories work, it was not. Then the generations of personal contact that the wealthy New England employer and his family had had with black servants might have caused the experiences that the black servant had with the employer to be more humane than those of the needed but ironically unwelcome Irish factory worker.[5]

The rise of an industrial economy brought different experiences to black and white workers. The possibility that these different experiences contributed to the tensions between the two groups cannot be overlooked. It is interesting that the town that antebellum black writers praised as an exemplar of humane race relations was New Bedford, Massachusetts. Both Frederick Douglass and William C. Nell noted how church and school were integrated in that seafaring town, how the racial frictions so strident in other places were lesser there. New Bedford was a town whose economic life centered on an older, pre-nineteenth-century enterprise, whaling. In nineteenth-century New England, it was the maritime trades that came the closest to providing a measure of occupational equality for blacks. Eighteenth-century black men had been mariners as slaves, freedmen, and runaways. The work was tough and dangerous; it could separate a man from his family for months, maybe years, sometimes forever. Perhaps black men could get jobs on ships because conditions were so harsh that it was hard to find men willing to go to sea. Certainly the foothold that blacks had gained in the seafaring trades in the eighteenth century caused a number of black men in coastal New England towns to be skilled mariners with a knowledge of the sea and ships that had passed down from one generation to another. In any event blacks in New Bedford were involved in an enterprise central to their town's economy. They were not part of that social and economic marginalization experienced by black in industrializing cities like Providence. This may partly explain why New Bedford was less segregated than other New England towns and cities.[6]

Political developments in the early nineteenth century also exerted a tremendous influence on the course of race relations in the Northeast. Whether black men voted in sufficient number to determine the outcome of many antebellum elections is less important than the fact that many, including many leaders of the Democratic party, believed that they did. Democrats who championed the rights of working-class whites to vote, while pressing with equal vigor for elimination of black suffrage, did so for explicitly political reasons. Like the Rhode Island Whigs who enfranchised blacks and blocked the access of the foreign born to the polls, Democrats worked to ensure that their supporters would be able to vote and that their opponents would not.

The long-term effects of these early racial and political alignments deserve further exploration. Students of race relations in nineteenth-century northern cities have traditionally assumed that the reason for the often-strident conflicts between blacks and working-class whites was competition for jobs. This view has been particularly strong among those trying to explore the antagonisms between blacks and Irish immigrants. Certainly enough examples of the two groups competing for jobs can be found to make the viewpoint a viable one, but it should not be allowed to stand alone as the sole reason for the development and persistence of these antagonisms. Too little attention has been paid to the fact that the political party that the Irish attached their loyalties to, the Democrats, was a party that had developed a strong Negrophobic sense a good two decades before the potato famine propelled large numbers of Irish im-

migrants to American shores in the 1840s. Equally important
is that the political allies of blacks were frequently those who
were fearful and resentful of the growing immigrant population.
It is significant that Know-Nothings helped to desegregate public
schools in Massachusetts and that the *Providence Journal*, which
played a significant role in mobilizing the black vote in the 1840s,
was bitterly xenophobic. Intergroup tensions mirrored political
animosities.

Blacks and Irish immigrants were not merely supporters of
two often bitterly competing political tendencies; they were
clients of the opposing political parties as well. Sometimes the
livelihoods of the two groups depended on their political client-
age. And in some ways their sense of acceptance by the larger
society was enhanced by their participation in the political process.
The black voter in New England or New York might be despised
and rebuffed year round, but a few weeks before an election, a
Whig or later a Republican politician might come to his church,
ask for his vote and by doing so, furnish one of the very few
examples of the civil equality that that black voter yearned for.
The Irish immigrant found a refuge in the Democratic party's
welcome, a relief in a land that many of them must have perceived as being overrun with snobbish Whigs and antipapist Know-
Nothings. The economic and sometimes psychological dependen-
cies of blacks and immigrants helped produce strong political
loyalties, loyalties that went beyond candidate and position. In
that light it is little wonder that animosities developed between
the two groups.

Politics and many of the other forces that helped to shape and
define modern American society also helped develop and exacer-
bate racial tensions in nineteenth-century America. These forces
and the changes that they brought about held out the hope
of better lives for average working people. The opening of the
West increased opportunities for landholding; common schools
allowed the children of poor and working-class families to receive
an education; universal manhood suffrage turned large numbers
of men into participants in the political process; the factory
allowed families to augment their incomes, put workers into
new and more independent relationships with the upper classes,
and opened new occupations and opportunities for working-

class people. These developments furnished evidence to large numbers of people that change was possible. Beginning in post-Revolutionary America, these new orderings of social, economic and political activities further convinced a people who had alrea had substantial experience in altering traditional arrangements that they need not be prisoners of past traditions that set artificial barriers on their ability to improve their lives.

The realization that life could be made better helped spur efforts to remove obstructions to individual and group progress. In Rhode Island, a curious combination of economic moderniza tion, the desire to better the conditions of ordinary working people, and an effort to formally define an inferior status for blacks came about at the same time. Early in the nineteenth century, workingmen's movements began to develop. In 1811, the first of many attempts to expand the suffrage beyond the freeholders began. That was also the first year that a legislative attempt to disenfranchise blacks occurred. By 1821, a convention was held to examine the question of the expansion of the suffrage. The convention was mainly supported by Providence and other industrializing towns.[7]

It was no mere coincidence of the history of Rhode Island or the northeastern United States that the transition to an industrial economy was accompanied by increased political and social ferment. In many societies, industrial development has influenced people to view class relationships and the social order in a new light. Societies undergoing the transition from preindustrial to industrial economies have often seen increased manifestations of working-class dissatisfaction and working-class consciousness. The change from older, paternalistic ways of organizing work and management to newer, less personal arrangements and the shift from individual tasks to regimented group labor have frequently contributed to a sense of alienation a sense that has spawned organizations of workers seeking to better their conditions. The social and political effects of industrial development have not been confined solely to those actually employed in factories. Factories have stimulated urban growth. Large concentrations of people in working-class and poor neighborhoods have enabled factory workers and thos working in other sectors of the economy to contrast their conditions and to join together in common cause. Urban growth and industrial development have also produced middle- and upper-class critics willing to explore and expose the harsher side of economic and social modernization. Writers like Charles Dickens, Emile Zola, and Upton Sinclair captured the tribulations of everyday life during periods of industrial growth. The reform spirit bred during industrialization has had important consequences. It was in the industrial period that western nations developed universal suffrage, the curtailment of capital punishment, asylums for the treatment of the insane, the concern with alcoholism's effects on the poor, and the improvement or institution of social welfare measures.

This transition from a traditional to a modern socioeconomic system and its resulting influence on people's attitudes about change had an effect on race relations. Some sociologists have addressed the general question of the relationships among modernization, social mobility and intergroup tensions. Pierre Van den Berghe in *Race and Racism* makes a useful distinction between paternalistic and competitive race relations. Briefly summarized, paternalistic race relations exist when superordinate groups and subordinate groups have sharply defined statuses; master and slave is the classic example. The economy of such a society is nonindustrial, usually agricultural, at most mercantile capitalist. Van den Berghe sees race relations under such a system as benign with accommodation on both sides as everyone recognizes and acquiesces in the social role that society has set out for them. The stereotypes that develop about the subordinate group in paternalistic society are "childish, immature, exuberant, uninhibited, lazy, impulsive, fun-loving, good humored, inferior but lovable." Also Van den Berghe argues that paternalistic societies have relatively constant patterns of racial prejudice.[8]

Van den Berghe sees a very different pattern of intergroup relations emerging in competitive societies; they are engaged in industrial enterprises. Their politics are democratic or quasi-democratic. Occupational mobility is possible in such societies because of the needs of industry. Unlike the paternalistic, aristocratic society that has been replaced, the competitive modern society must be rational. It must allocate status and prestige by achieved rather than ascribed criteria. In this type of society observable antagonisms between the races develop. The stereotypes of the subordinate group change. Instead of the previous nonthreatening stereotypes, new ones emerge. The subordinate group becomes "aggressive, uppity, insolent, over-sexed, dirty, inferior, despicable and dangerous." In this competitive society, superordinate aggression against the subordinate groups becomes routine. The race riot, the lynching, the pogrom all become aspects of the transition from paternalistic to competitive race relations.[9]

Van den Berghe's model has some value as an explanation of the transition that occurred in Providence during the slave and free eras. His model was designed to explain developments in plantation slave societies. One aspect of race relations that his model does not examine is the status of lower-class whites in a nonplantation, paternalistic system like the one that existed in eighteenth-century New England, though it could be argued that they might fit into the subordinate category under such conditions. He also failed to examine the role of harsh methods of social control in maintaining paternalistic societies, and he ignored the cases of strident resistance to the status quo that existed in plantation societies. Still, Van den Berghe's model shows the increase in tensions that occurs as societies shift from the clear subordination that occurs in paternalistic societies to the less-structured statuses of competitive societies. In many ways, this transition resembles the change that occurred in Europe in its evolution from feudal to industrial society. The parallel between the increase in class friction and the increase in racial conflict that Van den Berghe outlined can be properly drawn.[10]

While Van den Berghe's model predicts the sort of increase in racial tensions that occurred in nineteenth-century Providence it tells little about the kinds of interpersonal dynamics that contributed to the increased estrangement between blacks and working-class whites during that period. There is, however, a body of literature that goes beyond Van den Berghe's macro-analysis of societal change and looks at the kind of individual and group dynamics relevant to the phenomenon of perceived possibilities for social betterment and increased racial tension. This literature is concerned with the tensions that develop among those who feel that they may enhance their social or economic status. Some in such circumstances become anxious; they feel that their rise can occur only if others are prevented from moving upward. Others believe that only by making the distinctions between themselves and those who cannot or will not rise as sharp and as visible as possible will they be permitted to move up the social ladder. These sorts of attitudes have increased tensions even in uniracial social settings where potential candidates for upward mobility have taken pains to disassociate themselves from the attitudes and practices of their original reference groups and instead have adopted, often with a vengeance, the viewpoints of the groups that they have aspired to join. That this sort of attitudinal metamorphosis has created tremendous social tensions in once-homogeneous groups should help us to understand why the children and grandchildren of the eighteenth-century slaves and indentured servants, who drew few distinctions among themselves, were on different sides of an increasingly stringent color line in the nineteenth century.[11]

Americans in the early nineteenth century believed that they could improve their social status. Older beliefs about the immutability of class lines and the inevitability and desirability of class-based privileges were fading. In the North, blacks and whites were able to share in and act upon these new visions, but circumstances caused the two races to do so in different ways. White workers found that one way to achieve the mobility that they sought was to emphasize the social distinctions between themselves and blacks. It is dangerous and inevitably inaccurate to attempt to summarize the feelings of large numbers of very different people in a few sentences, but the often simultaneous movements toward greater egalitarianism for whites and sharper discrimination against blacks, the tendency toward an increasingly Herrenvolk democracy in early nineteenth-century America, seems to suggest that many who pressed the case for the improvement of conditions for working-class whites were saying, "You are discriminating against the wrong people; poor whites are white; they deserve to be included in this democracy that we are building. It is the Negroes who are different; they should be left out." This view caused many white workers to refuse to work alongside blacks. It was also the reason that the Rhode Island Suffrage Association rejected the alliance offered by Niger and Crummell. They feared the stigma that would come with an alliance with blacks.[12]

While white laborers were developing strategies for mobility that included erecting social boundaries between themselves and blacks, blacks were evolving their own strategies for individual and community betterment. The black progression from establishing separate households, to creating parallel social institutions, and ultimately to securing some political rights depended in part on demonstrating the respectability of and the adherence to middle-class values by the black community. One of the earliest black institutions in Providence, the African Union Meeting House, depended in its earlier years on white philanthropy. Patterns of black employment reinforced traditional dependent relations with upper-class whites. A respectable image on the part of blacks was necessary to secure the sort of assistance that enabled black institutions to provide cultural, social, and political leadership for the community. It was also necessary for the maintenance of the livelihoods of many.

This need to demonstrate respectability caused blacks to attempt to put social distance between themselves and the rougher elements of the white community. Those upwardly mobile blacks who were at the center of black social and political movements strongly felt this necessity. During slavery, when the majority of blacks saw only a life of bondage ahead of them, participating with lower-class whites in the general uproar of street life might be a welcome respite from the burdens of bondage. When the possibilities of home owning, church membership, even political participation unfolded, rowdiness became a threat, jeopardizing such aspirations. To a much greater extent than was the case with working-class whites, black advancement depended on group advancement and group image. A working-class white man might move from his original status to a higher one without having to defend the respectability of the group that he came from. For a black man such a transition was largely impossible. Either the group was deemed worthy, in which case new rights might be extended, as happened in the Rhode Island reenfranchisement of 1842, or the group would be unworthy and no member of the group, however accomplished, would be accorded additional rights. Even foreign-born whites, who were subject to fierce anti-pathies, did not face this sort of all-or-nothing situation. An Irishman fortunate enough to become wealthy or perhaps one who became a Protestant might find himself in very different circumstances from the masses of immigrants. An immigrant's son would be a native-born white man, with all of the legal privileges that that entailed. But for black leaders in an environment like antebellum Providence's, only a vigorous defense of the worthiness of the entire group would allow an individual to rise.

In Providence, one of the first signs of the tensions between laboring-class blacks and whites was conflict between respectable, status-seeking black families and sailors. Generally white seamen had a reputation for tolerance in regard to race relations; they were more willing to work alongside blacks than most whites. Despite this the 1820s and 1830s was a time of tension between black home owners and white sailors. The Olney Street riot of 1831 was in part a confrontation between these two groups. A partial explanation of this confrontation is the resentment that sailors had toward the more respectable black home owners.

Olney Street, like Hardscrabble, was a combination vice area and residential area for respectable black families. These families were extremely uncomfortable with the vice-ridden milieu in which they were forced to live. There were daily incidents between black residents and sailors in these areas. A number of black landlords refused to rent to sailors. The struggling working-class black families of Olney Street strove to sharpen the social boundaries between themselves and the rowdy sailors who frequented the bars, dance halls, and houses of prostitution on that street. The Olney Street riot started after a clash between white and black sailors and the shooting of a white sailor by a bartender. Brown noted: "They [the sailors] warned the better class of colored people to move out, then went on with their work of destruction, calling on men of like principles, from other towns, to help."[13]

Subsequent events reinforced and increased the patterns of conflict between working-class whites and blacks. Blacks, when pressing for their rights, would note that their industriousness, temperance, and other civic virtues were greater than those of working-class whites. The Irish would press for the elimination of the property qualification for the foreign born, with the argument that if blacks could vote without property, they certainly should be entitled to do so. The events and the memory of the Dorr war, of course, contributed to the exacerbation of tensions between the two groups.

The patterns, tendencies, and alignments that developed in northeastern cities like Providence persisted long after the actors who staged this drama passed from the scene. They continued not only in the older cities of the Northeast, but in the newer cities of the Midwest and Far West. Racial conflict is no recent twentieth-century import to the industrial North. It has deep roots in the region. We need to know more about how the institutional loyalties that blacks and whites developed in antebellum cities like Providence not only deepened the racial divisions of their day but those of succeeding generations as well. If the Democratic party was antiblack because a small number of black voters in New York and New England voted against it before the Civil War, did that hostility deepen as blacks throughout the North, not to mention the South, supported the party of Lincoln in postbellum America? Did that political hostility cause urban machines to transmit racial hostility to the waves of new Americans who came to the country throughout the nineteenth and much of the twentieth century? Was it significant that Irish immigrants to cities like Providence were Catholics and blacks were Protestants? Did that help reinforce patterns of separation between two working-class peoples? Did their absence from the factory until well into the twentieth century cause black workers to cling to premodern attitudes about class and labor long after they had become dysfunctional in a modern industrial economy? And what is perhaps the most important question, were the separate churches, political cultures and work places socializing vehicles where black and white could inform newcomers from Europe and the American South of the patterns of racial interaction in northern cities? If we start to explore the connections between the patterns that developed in the antebellum North and their later persistence and extension, we will have a better sense of the truly national nature of racial strife in this society.

But to do that we will have to turn back to the sorts of choices that blacks in places like antebellum Providence made and those that were made for them. Spurred on by the nineteenth-century belief that the present could be made better and the future better still, they worked to advance themselves and their community. The forces of social change that helped create discord among laboring-class people also helped foster the development of a community among the Afro-Yankees of Providence. The hostility of the larger society made group solidarity a prerequisite to any sort of betterment of either the individual or the collective condition. That was a lesson that would be relearned and repeated long after the death in 1859 of James Howland, Rhode Island's last slave.

Notes

1. Edwin M. Snow, *Census of Rhode Island, 1865* p. xlvi.

2. Frederick Jackson Turner, *The Frontier in American History* (New York: H. Holt and Company, 1920).

3. Leon F. Litwack, *North of Slavery*, pp. 64-112.

4. For a good account of the free Negro's status in antebellum Louisiana, see Ira Berlin, *Slaves without Masters*, pp. 108-32.

5. Sidney Ratner, James H. Soltow, and Richard Sylla, *The Evolution of the American Economy: Growth Welfare and Decision Making* (New York: Basic Books, 1979); Stephan Thernstrom, *Poverty and Progress: Social Mobility in a Nineteenth Century City* (Cambridge: Harvard University Press, 1964), pp. 60-61.

6. Frederick Douglass, *Life and Times of Frederick Douglass* (New York: Collier Macmillan, Ltd., 1962), pp. 206-12. New Bedford was not totally free of the kind of color prejudice that had developed elsewhere in New England. Douglass noted how he was prevented from working as a caulker in New Bedford because white caulkers threatened to quit if he was hired. He also noted how the New Bedford Lyceum did not allow blacks to attend lectures. Still, the fact that New Bedford's public schools were integrated long before Massachusetts's school desegregation law of 1855 is indicative of the generally higher degree of racial tolerance found in New Bedford when compared to other areas of New England at the time.

7. Jacob Frieze, *A Concise History of the Efforts to Obtain an Extension of Suffrage in Rhode Island.* For two valuable discussions of Rhode Island's transition from a maritime to an industrial economy, see Peter J. Coleman, *The Transformation of Rhode Island, 1790-1860*, and Joseph

Brennan, *Social Conditions in Industrial Rhode Island: 1820-1860* (Washington, D.C.: Catholic University, 1940).

8. Pierre Van den Berghe, *Race and Racism* (New York: John Wiley and Sons, 1967), pp. 31-33.

9. Ibid.

10. One of the difficulties with Van den Berghe's paternalistic model is that it was heavily influenced by Stanley Elkins's Sambo theory. See Elkins, *Slavery, A Problem in American Institutional and Intellectual Life* (New York: Grosset and Dunlap, 1963). This influence caused Van den Berghe to construct a model of paternalistic race relations that has, perhaps, overemphasized the role internalization of subordinate groups and the consequent benevolence of superordinate groups.

11. The social science literature treating the relationship between the possibility of social mobility and intragroup and intergroup tension is extensive. Two of the more important contributions have been T. W. Adorno et al., *The Authoritarian Personality* (New York: W. W. Norton, 1969), p. 272, and Robert K. Merton, *Social Theory and Social Structure* (New York: Free Press, 1968), pp. 319, 344. Merton's discussion of the tensions that developed in U.S. Army units during World War II when some recruits perceived the possibility of promotion is particularly valuable. See also Fred B. Silberstein and Melvin Seeman, "Social Mobility and Prejudice," *American Journal of Sociology* 65 (November 1959): 258-64; D. Stanley Eitzen, "Status Inconsistency and Wallace Supporters in a Midwestern City," *Social Forces* 48 (June 1970): 492-98; David R. Segal and David Knoke, "Social Mobility, Status Inconsistency and Partisan Realignment in the United States," *Social Forces* 47 (December 1968): 154-57; Joseph Lopreato, "Upward Social Mobility and Political Orientation," *American Sociological Review* 32 (August 1967): 582-86.

12. Students of race relations might find a framework that has been developed in the sociology of deviance valuable in explaining shifting racial attitudes. The concept of boundary maintenance (the idea that a group gains a sense of identity and group cohesion by redefining what it considers deviant and normal in the light of changing circumstances) is applicable to race relations. Just as the practice of defining a new form of deviant behavior and mobilizing the group against it can heighten group solidarity and a sense of group values, a new and more stringent emphasis on racial differences can have a similar effect. See Emile Durkheim, *The Rules of Sociological Method* (New York: Free Press, 1966), pp. 65-69, and Kai T. Erikson, *Wayward Puritans: A Study in the Sociology of Deviance* (New York: John Wiley and Sons, 1966).

13. Brown, *Life of Brown*, p. 95.

ESSAY ON
SELECTED SOURCES

Primary Sources

The availability of specific information about blacks in Providence tends to mirror the growth of the black community in that city. Unaffected by the virulent proslavery and antislavery debates that would generate volumes of polemical, autobiographical, and travel literature on nineteenth-century southern slavery, colonial Providence had relatively little to say about its slave population. What survives from the colonial era tends to be fragmentary information rarely meant to explain the condition of blacks. As the blacks moved into freedom and began establishing their own institutions, they left records of their efforts by pleading the cause of equal rights and chronicling their activities. Finally, as the community grew and began to have a greater impact on general politics, more whites began to note various aspects of black life in Providence.

Official colonial records provide a glimpse into eighteenth-century black life. The *Rhode Island Colonial Records, The Early Records of the Town of Providence, The Colonial Records of Connecticut,* and *The Records of the Boston Selectmen* all document problems connected with the social control of the black slave and white servant populations. Generally these sources were concerned with blacks only when they impinged on the social order or as slaves related to commerce. On occasion individual blacks would show up as part of larger colonial enterprises. Connecticut and Rhode Island muster rolls, the latter compiled by Howard Chapin in *A List of Rhode Island Soldiers and Sailors in the Old French and Indian War*, furnish evidence of black participation in that early American conflict. *The Rhode Island Census of 1774* furnishes information about slaveholding patterns, though it is of little value to the researcher interested in finding out about family life or the occupations of blacks in eighteenth-century Providence.

Two collections of documents that are invaluable for researchers looking at blacks in colonial New England, and indeed for other facets of Afro-American history, are Elizabeth Donnan's *Documents Illustrative of the History of the Slave Trade to America*, vol. 3, and Helen T. Catterall's *Judicial Cases Concerning American Slavery and the Negro*, vol. 4. The documents in the former volume provide valuable information about the slave trade, the economics of slavery, and the evolving reaction of colonial New England society to the trade. Catterall's compilation of cases documents relations between blacks and whites in colonial New England. The ability of blacks to sue in colonial New England courts is attested to by her collection of legal cases.

Colonial newspapers by and large did not report on events in their home cities. They were published weekly, generally covering foreign news or news of other colonies. Those studying blacks in colonial New England find the problem of using newspapers exacerbated because of the relatively small size of the black population. Advertisements provide the best information about slaves in New England. The *Providence Gazette* contained advertisements for runaway slaves and servants that provide interesting glimpses into the lives of these two groups. One rare and serendipitous find was an account of the Pope's Day riot that occurred in Boston in 1765, related in the *Boston Gazette*. This mention differed from the standard pattern in colonial New England newspapers of providing little information about local events and, of course, even less about the conditions of blacks.

Fortunately doing the history of slaves and free Negroes in colonial New England is not solely an exercise in researching the history of the inarticulate. *A Narrative of the Life and Adventures of Venture, A Native of Africa*, Venture Smith's autobiography, is an insider's intimate account of mid-eighteenth-century New England slave life. Smith's remarkable story is one of the earliest black writings in this country that discusses slavery and race relations. His discussion of his West African childhood, including his being captured as a slave, and his efforts to buy his freedom have a value for historians examining general Afro-American history. *The Autobiography of James Mars* is a helpful source for those wishing to look at the waning days of northern slavery and the emergence of free Negro society after northern emancipation.

The organizational activities of the emerging free Negro population furnish some of the best information about the activities and aspirations of the community. I would argue that anyone studying an essentially working-class black community like the one in Providence benefits from the writings of community leaders who themselves were manual laborers and small businessmen and who lived in close proximity to less articulate poor people. Unlike the often discussed, and in my opinion somewhat exaggerated, gulf between the working and articulate classes in white communities, the fact that black leaders came from and were to a large extent advocates and apologists for a working class gives their writings a usefulness in studying black working-class communities that is often absent for researchers examining white working-class communities.

The Proceedings of the Free African Union Society and the African Benevolent Society Newport, Rhode Island, 1780-1824 edited by William H. Robinson, contains the records of two of the earliest organizations formed by blacks in Rhode Island. The correspondence of these organizations tells quite a bit about the origins of free Negro culture in Rhode Island, the search for respectability, religiosity, and dependence on philanthropic whites. A valuable look at the founding of the first black church in Providence, *A Short History of the African Union Meeting House* is another source that shows the researcher how blacks formed organizations and the differences and similarities of those organizations with respect to their white counterparts. The *Minutes of a Convention of People of Color for the Promotion of Temperance in New England* furnishes a glimpse into a largely ignored chapter in both Afro-American history and the history of the American temperance movement.

An invaluable set of sources are the writings of those who participated in the struggle for equal rights. U.S. Congressional Report No. 546, "Interference in the Internal Affairs of Rhode Island," contains the statement of Alfred Niger and other black men from Providence who were pressing the cause of restoration of black voting rights. The school integration struggle produced two documents, *Will the General Assembly Put Down Caste Schools* and *To the Friends of Equal Rights in Rhode Island*, that show the development of a black political infrastructure that managed somewhat to loosen the patron-client ties that had been forged with aristocratic whites during the Dorr war. One autobiography, *The Life of George Henry*, details one person's participation in the school integration effort. Henry's autobiography is also an important source for those interested in seeing how black workers acquired property, often by exploiting the very racial discrimination designed to keep them in an inferior status.

Anyone researching the lives of black people in nineteenth-century Providence will quickly come to appreciate his or her debt to a remarkable individual: cobbler, community leader, and chronicler William J. Brown. *The Life of William J. Brown* is a firsthand history that preserves what otherwise might have been a forgotten memory of eighteenth-century black life in Rhode Island. Brown's autobiography, the early part of which preserves an oral tradition given him by his parents, is the only account by a black person that I am aware of that details relations between African slaves and the native Narragansetts. His autobiography is also important because it gives a firsthand account of the African elections in Rhode Island.

The primary value of Brown's narrative is his telling the event of his life. His account of his schooling, his early experiences in Providence's First Baptist Church, and his working for and living with a white family as a child is a source on what it was like for a black child to grow up in early nineteenth-century New England that should be valuable for students of Afro-American history, New England history, and the history of child rearing. Brown's leadership in community struggles is recounted in his

autobiography. His discussion of how he helped to organize the
black vote for the Whig party is an important resource for those
interested in studying the history of black political behavior.
Although the allegiance of blacks to the Whig party in the antebellum North has long been recognized by historians, little attention has been paid to the motives and aspirations of the
antebellum black voter. Brown's autobiography suggests that
for some free Negroes, the vote took on a life of its own, independent of the abolitionist effort and the larger political currents of the times.

Every historian is aware of some unfortunate occurrence that
has resulted in the destruction of a potentially valuable primary
source. Sometimes serendipity greets the historian, the unlikely
source, telling a story usually denied the researcher. Frances
McDougall's two biographies of a black laundress, *Memoirs of
Eleanor Eldridge* and *Eleanor's Second Book*, provide a life
story of the sort of person of whom we rarely get a glimpse in
most historical studies. Illiterate, black, a menial laborer, a woman, and not a participant in any major social movement, Eleanor
Eldridge would have been just a name on a census schedule to
the student of nineteenth-century Providence except for her
having been cheated and for Frances McDougall's efforts to help
her recoup her losses by writing her biographies. Often maudlin,
hoping to evoke sympathy for the wronged Eldridge, these
biographies supply the kind of important detail about one life
that leads to speculation about similar lives. McDougall's biographies are important social histories, supplying information
about the African king's elections, black life in early nineteenth-
century Rhode Island, and, of course, the remarkable story of
Eleanor Eldridge's trials and successes.

Generally the white community tended to notice Providence
blacks as a problem. The Moses Brown Papers show the Quaker
reformer's involvement as a protector of newly freed and about
to be emancipated blacks. In the early nineteenth century, the
Providence Gazette continued to ignore day-to-day life in the
black community. The Hardscrabble riot with its large-scale
disruption and destruction attracted some attention from the
Providence Gazette. Because of the times in which it was published, the *Providence Journal* provided more information

about free Negro life in Providence. A daily paper, the *Providence Journal* covered the Olney Street riot. The *Journal's* Whig sympathies and the evolution of Rhode Island's political history caused it to pay attention to the black community as it sought to bring blacks into the political process on the Whig side.

The Dorr war naturally generated a large number of documents relevant to those interested in studying the efforts of blacks and working-class whites to attain suffrage and the efforts of conservatives to maintain aristocratic power and privilege. The Rhode Island Suffrage Association's newspaper, *New Age and Constitutional Advocate*, is valuable for those interested in looking at the conflict from the association's point of view. That paper is an excellent source for those interested in exploring the range of views on race relations and abolition found within the Suffrage Association. Those interested in obtaining a firsthand view of the efforts of white workingmen to obtain suffrage will also find Seth Luther's *An Address on the Right of Free Suffrage* valuable. A contemporary view of suffrage extension in Rhode Island that has considerable value as a primary source is Jacob Frieze's *A Concise History of the Efforts to Obtain an Extension of Suffrage in Rhode Island.*

Black and abolitionist partisans outside of Rhode Island noticed the Providence Negro community, applauding its triumphs and advising the community on various courses of action. Several newspapers, including the *Liberator*, the *National Anti-Slavery Standard*, and the *North Star*, covered the Dorr rebellion and black political behavior after reenfranchisement. Because the reenfranchisement was one of the more spectacular successes of the antebellum northern equal-rights movement, black and abolitionist leaders paid attention to events in Providence. Massachusetts civil rights advocate William C. Nell in his history of black participation in the American military, *The Colored Patriots of the American Revolution*, noted Rhode Island's sponsorship of a black militia company. Like others who took note of the company, he was arguing for the right of free Negroes elsewhere to participate in state militias.

Travelers' accounts are among the staples of the narrative historian's diet. American slavery and race relations fascinated foreign visitors and was the principal concern of many who wrote about their travels. Alexis de Tocqueville's observations on American race relations in *Democracy in America* was one of the earliest efforts to describe the different racial cultures in the North and South. By and large, travelers did not notice Providence's black community, due to Providence's being relatively out of the way and the small size of the Providence black population. J. S. Buckingham took brief notice of Negro life in Providence in his account, *America, Historical, Statistic and Descriptive.* British abolitionist E. S. Abdy did not write about blacks in Providence in his *Journal of a Residence and Tour in the United States.* Nonetheless, his book provides important insights into race relations and free black life in northern cities. Of special interest for purposes of this study was Abdy's discussion of Democratic reactions to the Federalist sympathies of black voters in New York.

Recent developments in historiography have reiterated the value of governmental statistical records to the social historian. Like traditional literary sources, these government records are of mixed value, reflecting the purposes, biases, and sensitivities of agencies and recorders. United States manuscript census schedules provide important records of the economic and family circumstances of ordinary people. Federal censuses before 1850 were too inexact, particularly in their coverage of blacks, to be of much value to those doing social and economic research. The censuses of 1850 and 1860 provide important data for the historian, though one must bear in mind that there was a probable underenumeration of the black population, stemming from the reluctance of fugitive slaves to be counted by census takers and because a considerable number of black men who had families in Providence were probably searching for work elsewhere.

Rhode Island state and local records are less satisfactory as sources of information about masses of people than the manuscript federal censuses, but they are useful auxiliary sources. *The Providence City Directories* provide less information than the censuses; they covered only heads of households or owners of businesses, and they did not indicate race. *The Rhode Island State Census of 1865* is a valuable supplement useful for those wishing to compare the white and black and native and foreign-born populations. *The Providence City Census of 1855* gives aggregate information on occupations within Providence and is also useful because it has reprints of previous city censuses, making it possible to trace rates of white and black population growth. *The Providence Tax Lists* had a special section for "people of color," enhancing the usefulness of the lists for this research. Probate records were helpful in providing a glimpse into the day-to-day living patterns of some of Providence's black property holders. In many ways, however, these probate records were less revealing than they might have been for a researcher studying a contemporary white community. Those listed in the probate records were the community leaders and property holders mentioned by the narrative sources. Because of the greater prosperity of the white population, researchers would be likely to find more probate records for whites, including records of people who were not articulate community leaders.

The sorts of primary sources available to the student of a particular people are a reflection of the various circumstances of that people and the larger society in which they lived. Black efforts to be included in the practices and institutions of antebellum America caused black activists, as well as white sympathizers and critics, to write describing the circumstances of northern blacks. Such northern cities as Boston, New York, Philadelphia, and Rochester produced a black literary and journalistic elite in the antebellum period. Providence did not produce a black newspaper or house a major black essayist. Instead the story of Providence's black community is told by the ordinary men who spent their lives struggling to carve out a place for themselves in American society. In many ways the history of free Negroes in Providence is better memorialized by the writings of the ordinary residents with their parochial concerns than it might have had Providence been the home of some of the more illustrious black persons of the antebellum era. The day-to-day concerns, the desire to celebrate relatively minor triumphs, the quest for recognition, led to a home-grown literature that provides an invaluable foundation for those studying everyday black life in antebellum Providence.

Secondary Sources

There is a long history of writing about black life in the pre-Civil War North; unfortunately this writing has not yet had the impact on scholarly and popular discussions of the evolution of American race relations that it should. This is unfortunate because this long historiographic tradition has much to tell us about the origins of northern racial conflict, the importance of which continues to become clearer. The historiography of northern black life is an important part of the larger Afro-American and regional historiographies that are relevant to this study.

When James Mars wrote his autobiography in 1868, he said that he did so to remind people that slavery had existed in Connecticut. Many others who have written on New England and northern slavery have done so with similar motivations. During the nineteenth century, New England writers, largely influenced by the abolitionist and equal rights movements, began the exploration of the region's slave past, often with polemical as well as historical purposes in mind. One of the earliest efforts, George H. Moore's *Notes on the History of Slavery in Massachusetts*, was an attempt to remind Massachusetts of its past participation in slavery and slaving. Another purpose was served by Caroline Hazard's study of her family's involvement in Narragansett plantation slavery, *College Tom: A Study of Life in Narragansett in the XVIII Century*. Her purpose was to show eighteenth-century planter Thomas Harard's abolitionist activities and the benign nature of Rhode Island slavery. Black activist William C. Nell's work, *The Colored Patriots of the American Revolution*, was in part an attempt to buttress the New England black equal rights movement by recalling the role blacks from New England and other areas had played in the Revolution. Partly motivated by a desire to prevent the story of Rhode Island's black regiment from being used as an argument for civil rights, Rhode Island local historian Sidney S. Rider wrote *An Historical Inquiry Concerning the Attempt to Raise a Regiment of Slaves by Rhode Island*. Lorenzo Green's article "Some Observations on the Black Regiment of Rhode Island," was designed to counteract Rider's negative reporting of the efforts of Rhode Island black troops in the Revolution.

Other nineteenth-century studies remain the major examinations of slavery in local contexts. Orville H. Platt's essay, "Negro Governors," is still the foundation of any study of the black elections that occurred in colonial New England. Valuable as Platt's essay is, the researcher is still frustrated in attempting to use his article as a lead to primary sources because much of what Platt wrote was based on local tradition, especially the remembrances of people who participated in the last of the elec tions in the early nineteenth century. Of more general value is William Dawson Johnston's Slavery in *Rhode Island, 1755-1776*, which was accomplished by a fruitful exploration of the *Rhode Island Colonial Records* and various local histories. One of the first professional studies of slavery in a New England state was Bernard C. Steiner's *History of Slavery in Connecticut* Part of the Johns Hopkins studies of slavery in the various states done in the 1890s, his study was primarily a legal history, valuable for its examination of the law pertaining to slavery but less valuable as a social analysis.

Of course, one cannot discuss the secondary literature on slavery in New England without acknowledging the preeminenc of Lorenzo Johnston Greene's *The Negro in Colonial New England*. After Greene's study, the field of New England slavery would no longer be a curiosity, the nearly exclusive province of the antiquarian and local historian. Instead the field would large ly be defined by Greene's perceptions. Greene's survey of colon newspapers, state and local documents, local histories, and personal accounts was comprehensive, providing a gold mine for other researchers. One bibliographic deficiency in his study is that he did not incorporate the personal narratives of people like Venture Smith, James Mars, and William Brown. Despite this, Greene's work captures the flavor of life for New England master and slave, as well as others in colonial New England.

Other studies of American slavery raise questions that have importance for the New England specialist. Edgar J. McManus's *Black Bondage in the North* is primarily a legal history of slaver in the North; as such it has the strengths and deficiencies of that approach. Ulrich B. Phillips's *American Negro Slavery* brief ly treated northern slavery, though he regarded this treatment basically as background to the story of the plantation South that was his main concern. Richard C. Wade's history of urban slavery, *Slavery in the Cities*, raises important questions about social relations in slavery outside of the plantation context. Wade's thesis-that the urban context permitted slaves a degree of physical and personal independence unmatched on the plan-

tation--is helpful for those wishing to understand northern
slavery. Relations between slaves and white indentured servants
should be of interest to any student of colonial race relations.
Edmund Morgan's *American Slavery, American Freedom: The
Ordeal of Colonial Virginia* is a systematic examination of relations between the two laboring groups during the colonial era
that adds much to the discussions of the origins of American
race relations.

The role of the free Negro in nineteenth-century America's
evolving democratic order merits further attention. Dixon Ryan
Fox's 1917 essay, "The Negro Vote in Old New York," argued
that post-Civil War black political behavior was not solely the
result of Republican abolitionist activity but that it was rooted
in alliances and antagonisms forged in the early nineteenth century. His essay is an important beginning for anyone desiring to
explore black political activity in New York and the New England states in the early nineteenth century. Of less general importance is James Truslow Adams's "Disenfranchisement of
Negroes in New England." Adams's essay was less detailed and
informative than Fox's, though he did confirm Fox's view that
free Negro voters tended to have Federalist sympathies. His
essay is also interesting because he managed to uncover evidence
of blacks' voting in Connecticut and Rhode Island before black
disenfranchisement (1818 and 1822, respectively, in those states).
Lee Benson's *The Concept of Jacksonian Democracy* continues
Fox's discussion of the antebellum political history of black
New Yorkers. Benson essentially reaffirms Fox's perceptions of
the enmity between New York blacks and the Democratic party.

Leon Litwack's *North of Slavery* is the most comprehensive
study of the free Negro condition in the northern states. *North
of Slavery* does an important job of outlining the growth of formal legal restrictions against blacks. Because Litwack's study
was primarily a legal history and because he was discussing all
of the free states, the treatment was largely confined to legislative and judicial sources. His study does little social or economic
exploration of the conditions of free Negroes, except for what
the legal sources would tend to suggest. Given the general nature
of his work, that is clearly understandable because state and local
studies are necessary to probe social and economic data.

Rhode Island's black history has long attracted the attention of antiquarians, history enthusiasts, and, increasingly, profession historians. Charles A. Battle's *Negroes on the Island of Rhode Island* is an antiquarian study that has useful information on various phases of black life in Rhode Island. It is a frustrating study for historians to use because Battle did not footnote his sources, making replication and verification difficult. Julian Rammelkamp's "The Providence Negro Community, 1820-1841," was the first professional investigation of antebellum black life in Providence. Rammelkamp's study was particularly important because of his uncovering of sources; he was the first historian to use William J. Brown's autobiography. A valuable account of the activities of Providence blacks during the Dorr rebellion is "Reenfranchisement of Rhode Island Negroes" by J. Stanley Lemons and Michael McKenna. Their article concentrated on the Dorr conflict and told little of the efforts of blacks and poor whites to obtain the vote before the conflict. Lawrence Grossman's "George T. Downing and Desegregation of Rhode Island Public Schools, 1855-1866," is a good examina tion of Downing's role in the school desegregation effort. Because Grossman concentrates on Downing, his article is not particularly helpful for those interested in the role Providence's indigenous black political infrastructure played in the desegrega tion effort. One local history, Irving Bartlett's *From Slave to Citizen, The Story of the Negro in Rhode Island*, is a general history of blacks in Rhode Island; most of its information on the nineteenth century comes from Rammelkamp's study. A recent addition to the literature, William H. Robinson's *Blacks in Nineteenth Century Rhode Island: An Overview*, points to the rich array of sources available to those interested in studyir the lives of black people in Rhode Island.

The Dorr war's importance to the development of black life in Rhode Island is obvious, and historians of Rhode Island, loc and national, have paid some, albeit minor, attention to the bla role in the conflict. Arthur May Mowry's study, *The Dorr War*, completed in 1901, was sympathetic to the Whig side and used black reenfranchisement to argue the moral superiority of the law and order forces. Two modern studies, George M. Dennison

The Dorr War and Marvin Gettleman's *The Dorr Rebellion*, present more sympathetic portraits of the Suffrage party. Neither concentrates on the rebellion's effects on blacks, though they do give a good outline of black actions in the Dorr war.

Anyone undertaking a study of a black community, or indeed any other social history, should be familiar with some of the new social history studies that have been undertaken since World War II. Emphasizing quantifiable sources (censuses, city directories, probate, and vital statistic records) and deemphasizing the sources of the old social history (letters, diaries, autobiographies, and oral tradition), these newer studies frequently promise to separate folklore from history and provide more accurate pictures of the past. These studies have tended to ask questions suitable to the sources they have chosen: quantifiable questions, questions about occupational mobility, property accumulation, in-migration and out-migration, and family and household size. Generally these studies have not examined attitudes, social relations, and the culture of the peoples they have been examining. Those writing the new social history have tended either to ignore such qualitative questions, claiming that literary sources are either unavailable for common working people or that they suffer from an upper-class bias, or to use the qualitative findings of other social historians as hypotheses to be tested by their quantitative data. These efforts have given us important information about populations and economic circumstances in the past, though they have done something less than present a full portrait of ordinary people in the past. In part the difficulty with some of these works is the assumption that the poor and working classes have been consistently inarticulate in the past. Thus some historians have taken an assumption that is doubtless correct for those studying peasants in premodern Europe, probably correct for Western Europe and the United States at the beginnings of the industrial revolution, but dubious for Western Europe and the United States since the early years of the nineteenth century, and used that as the reasons for confining their investigation to quantifiable sources.

Stephan Thernstrom's *Poverty and Progress* and *The Other Bostonians* are useful models of this new history approach. Both are mobility studies that have emphasized quantitative records. Thernstrom's exploitation of U.S. censuses and other quantifiable sources has produced two important portraits of working-class mobility. His methodology has slighted qualitative strategies, thus not allowing his working-class subjects to inform us about their lives. This is an especially important consideration for those interested in studies of black communities because so much of the qualitative story is yet to be explored. Nonetheless, the techniques of the new social history are valuable ways of analyzing trends for large populations and have produced important discoveries for those interested in studying black communities.

Social histories of black communities have been an important part of the effort to develop Afro-American history since W.E.B. Du Bois's groundbreaking study, *The Philadelphia Negro*, completed in 1896. Du Bois's study set the major parameters for those who would undertake similar studies in other cities. His study synthesized historical scholarship with newly developed sociological techniques and was especially valuable for his pioneeing use of the census to delineate the socioeconomic circumstances of Philadelphia's black community. One of the earliest studies of black life in urban New England was John Daniels's *In Freedom's Birthplace: A Study of the Boston Negroes* (1917) His work furnishes a basic history of the efforts of Boston Negroes to obtain equal treatment in various facets of political and civil life, but it contains little information about the social and economic circumstances of blacks in Boston. One of the more important examinations of black life in a nineteenth-century northern city is Robert Austin Warner's *New Haven Negroes*. Warner utilized a wide variety of sources—literary, including those of black community leaders, as well as U.S. census sources and city directories. *New Haven Negroes* is sensitive to the effects of time on race relations. One of the strengths of Warner's book is that he does perceive the correlation between the growth of Jacksonian democracy and racism in the North in the early nineteenth century. Warner's discussion of black occupational position in New Haven and how it was affected by European immigration is especially valuable.

Modern studies of nineteenth-century black communities provide useful contrasts with this one. John Blassingame's *Black*

New Orleans, 1860-1880 suggests that many of the social processes that occurred among southern blacks after the Civil War
were similar to those of free Negroes in the North earlier in the
century. The struggle to establish an independent black family
life, the development of black social institutions, and efforts to
secure equal political rights have important similarities in northern and southern contexts. Yet post-Civil War New Orleans differed from antebellum Providence. New Orleans had a larger
Negro population, and differences between blacks and mulattoes
were clear. A distinct Negro upper class had developed in New
Orleans, the French-speaking mulattoes who had been free in
the antebellum period. The differences between the development of black communities and race relations in southern and
northern cities are important and deserve more comprehensive
attention.

Another important study is David Katzman's *Before the
Ghetto: Black Detroit in the Nineteenth Century.* Katzman's
profile of the development of Detroit's black community explains racial discrimination in terms of the concept of caste.
I think that his use of the term caste illustrates a difficulty that
social scientists and historians have when discussing American
black-white relations: the problem of comparison and utiliza-
tion of social theory developed in other contexts. Thinking of
American race relations as class relations is simply inadequate.
Blacks with sharply contrasting socioeconomic, educational,
and philosophical differences have been lumped together throughout too much of American history for conventional notions of
class to retain any validity. Indeed, I am somewhat persuaded
by Carl N. Degler's argument found in *Neither Black nor White*
that it has been white America's unwillingness to recognize
class differences among Negroes that has helped further development of group consciousness among the U.S. black population.
Katzman and others have substituted the concept of caste, original-
ly borrowed from students of Indian social structure, for class as
a means of explaining racial stratification in American society. At
first the caste strategy appears more promising than the highly
problematic class concept. Caste does not exclude the possibility
of class differences within different caste groups; blacks at various
times have used the term to describe the rigid discrimination that

has occurred; and, finally, caste seems to be the best means of describing the nearly inescapable hereditary racial barriers that have existed for most of American history.

The concept's difficulty lies with the problem of mutual acceptance by the putative castes. The classic caste system of the Indian subcontinent, rooted in the Hindu religion, involved an acceptance by subordinate as well as superordinate castes. Black adoption of American culture coupled with the culture's democratic and egalitarian values has prevented a black internalization and acceptance of caste roles. Indeed a substantial portion of the history of free Afro-Americans has been the attempt to eradicate discriminatory barriers erected by the larger society. The inconsistency of American ideals and a caste system has also influenced the behavior of white Americans. Racial discrimination has been a striking anomaly in a society that has professed egalitarianism. It has been an embarrassment, or as Gunnar Myrdal termed it, "an American dilemma." This too is inconsistent with the sort of cultural acceptance necessary to have a true caste system.

Practitioners of the new social and economic history are also starting to make significant contributions to the study of Afro-American communities in the North in the nineteenth century. The work of Theodore Hershberg and his associates in the Philadelphia Social History Project, some of which is contained in the essays found in *Philadelphia*, shows how interdisciplinary teamwork, social science concepts, and quantitative methods can illuminate the study of black life in a northern city in the nineteenth century. The revolution in computer technology in both hardware and software that has occurred over the last two decades has permitted a comprehensive mining of manuscript census and other quantifiable data bases that has allowed controlled comparisons of different demographic and economic indices of black populations and different subsections of white populations. This has proved to be an invaluable asset for those wishing to contrast the socioeconomic development of blacks and immigrant groups in cities. Important as the new methodologies will doubtless be in future reconstructions of the black past, it is to be hoped that these strategies will not be done to the exclusion of uncovering the qualitative stories of ordinary black people who lived in the cities of the past.

Two recent studies of black life in Boston indicate that the methodological strategies of the new social history can be fruitfully combined with that concern for the cultural values and outlook of a people that has long been the hallmark of good social history. *Black Bostonians* by James Horton and Lois Horton details the richness of black community life in antebellum Boston. That study is especially insightful in its detailing of the role of the lower strata of the community in the struggle to halt the return of fugitive slaves to bondage. Elizabeth Hafkin Pleck's *Black Migration and Poverty* is more interested in the demographic and economic issues of the new economic and social history, but she nonetheless manages to paint significant portraits of individuals acting within social and economic processes. Of special value is her contrasting of the cultures of native black Bostonians with those of southern migrants.

There is one area that students of black life in the nineteenth-century North should pay more attention to in the future: politics. The fact that blacks from their earliest history as voters voted against the Democratic party and continued to do so throughout the nineteenth and indeed much of the twentieth century had to have a profound impact on race relations in northern cities. Exploring the possibility of politically generated antagonisms between blacks and immigrants, who were often clients of the Democratic party, could add a new dimension to our understanding of the development of race relations in the North. It is one of many hypotheses we must build and test if we are to come to grips with the truly national nature of the American dilemma.

SELECTED
BIBLIOGRAPHY

Primary Sources

Autobiographies, Biographies, Diaries,
Papers, and Travel Accounts

Abdy, E. S. *Journal of a Residence and Tour in the United States. 3 vols.* London: John Murray, 1835.

Belknap Papers. *Massachusetts Historical Collection.* Fifth Series. Vol. 3.

Brissot, J. P. *Travels in the United States.* London, 1794.

Brown, Moses. "Moses Brown Manumission Papers." Moses Brown Manuscript Papers. Providence: Rhode Island Historical Society.

Brown, William J. *The Life of William J. Brown.* Providence: H. H. Brown, 1883.

Buckingham, J. S. *American Historical, Statistic and Descriptive.* Vol. 3. London, 1841.

Dexter, Franklin B., ed. *The Literary Diary of Ezra Stiles.* 2 vols. New York: Scribner & Sons, 1901.

Douglass, Frederick. *Life and Times of Frederick Douglass.* New York: Collier Books, 1962.

Dwight, Timothy. *Travels in New England and New York.* Cambridge: Harvard University Press, 1923.

Farrel, John T., ed. *The Superior Court Diary of William Samuel Johnson.* Washington, D.C., 1942.

Goe, C. C. *The Works of Jonathan Edwards—The Great Awakening.* New Haven: Yale University Press, 1972.

Henry, George. *Life of George Henry, Together with a Brief History of the Colored People in America.* Providence: H. I. Gould & Co., 1894.

Huntington Papers. *Connecticut Historical Society Collections.* Vol. 20. Hartford, 1923.

King, Dan. *The Life and Times of Thomas Wilson Dorr.* Boston, 1859.

Law Papers. Vol. 2, 1745-1746. *Connecticut Historical Society Collections.* Vol. 13. Hartford, 1914.

McDougall, Frances. *Memoirs of Eleanor Eldridge.* Providence: B. T. Albro, 1839.

——. *Eleanor's Second Book.* Providence: B. T. Albro, 1847.

Mars, James. *Life of James Mars, A Slave Born and Sold in Connecticut.* Hartford, 1868.

Martineau, Harriet. *Society in America.* Vol. 2. London, 1837.

Smith, Venture. *A Narrative of the Life and Adventures of Venture Smith, A Native of Africa.* Middletown, Conn.: J. S. Stuart, 1897.

Stevens, Charles Emery. *Anthony Burns, A History.* New York: Arno Press, 1969.

Tocqueville, Alexis de. *Democracy in America.* New York: Vintage Books, 1945.

Federal Records

Heads of Families First Census, 1790—Rhode Island. Washington, D.C.: Government Printing Office, 1908.

Lists of Black Servicemen Compiled from the War Department Collection of Revolutionary War Records. National Archives and Record Service, General Services Administration. Washington, D.C., 1974.

United States Bureau of the Census. 1790, 1800, 1810, 1820, 1830, 1840, 1850, and 1860 Censuses (manuscripts and published).

United States Congress, House, Select Committee Report No. 546 "Interference in the Internal Affairs of Rhode Island."

Newspapers

Boston Gazette, 1765.
Connecticut (New London) Journal, 1764.
Liberator, 1839-1858.
National Anti-Slavery Standard, 1843, 1844.
New Age and Constitutional Advocate, 1840-1842.
North Star, 1844-1848.
New Haven Chronicle, 1787.
New Haven Gazette, 1784-1785.
Non-Slave Holder, 1846.

Providence Gazette, 1763-1824.
Providence Journal, 1831-1865.

Pamphlets, Firsthand Histories, Institutional Records, and Documents

A Short History of the African Union Meeting House. Providence, 1821.
Annual Reports of the American Anti-Slavery Society. New York, 1856.
Bowen, Francis. *The Recent Contest in Rhode Island*. Boston: Otis, Broaders Co., 1844.
Catteral, Helen T. *Judicial Cases Concerning American Slavery and the Negro*. Vol. 4. Washington, D.C.: Carnegie Institution, 1932.
Clark, Thomas M. *The State of the Country, A Sermon Delivered in Grace Church Providence*. Providence, 1860.
Donnan, Elizabeth. *Documents Illustrative of the History of the Slave Trade in America*. Vol. 3. Washington, D.C.: Carnegie Institution, 1932.
Facts Involved in the Rhode Island Controversy. Boston: B. B. Mussey, 1842.
Freize, Jacob. *A Concise History of the Efforts to Obtain an Extension of Suffrage in Rhode Island*. Providence: B. F. Moore, 1842.
Goodell, William. *The Rights and Wrongs of Rhode Island*. Whiteboro, N.Y.: Oneica Press, 1842.
Hard Scrabble Calendar: Report of the Trials of Oliver Cummins, Nathaniel G. Metcalf, Gilbert Hines and Arthur Farrier. Providence, 1824.
Hazard, Thomas R. *An Appeal to the People of Rhode Island in Behalf of the Constitution and the Laws*. Providence, 1857.
King, Henry Melville, ed. *Historical Catalog of the Members of the First Baptist Church in Providence, Rhode Island*. Providence, 1908.
Luther, Seth. *An Address on the Right of Free Suffrage*. Providence: S. R. Weeden, 1833.
McDougall, Frances H. *Might and Right; By a Rhode Islander*. Providence: A. H. Stillwell, 1844.
Manuscript Records. Christ Church Episcopal. Providence, 1842.
Minutes of a Convention of People of Color for the Promotion of Temperance in New England. Providence, 1908.
Petition of Henry J. Duff and Others for an Alteration of the State Constitution. Providence: M. B. Young's Press, 1846.
Potter, Elisha R. *Considerations on the Rhode Island Question*. Boston: T. H. Webb, 1842.
Proceedings of the Anti-Slavery Convention of American Women. New York, 1838.
Providence Anti-Slavery Society. Providence, 1835.

Providence Association for the Benefit of Colored Children. *Annual Report* *1-12*. Providence, 1840-1851.

Report of the Executive Committee of the American Union 1836. Boston, 1836.

Robinson, William, ed. *The Proceedings of the Free African Union Society and the African Benevolent Society. Newport, Rhode Island, 1786 1824*. Providence: Urban League of Rhode Island, 1976.

To the Friends of Equal Rights in Rhode Island. Providence, 1857.

State and Local Records

Bartlett, John Russell, ed. *Records of the Colony of Rhode Island, and Providence Plantations in New England, 1856-1865*. Providence.

——. *Seventh Report of Births, Marriages and Deaths, 1859*. Providence: A. Cran & Greene, 1860.

Census of the Inhabitants of the Colony of Rhode Island, 1774. Providence Knowles, Anthony & Co., 1858.

Census of Providence, 1855. Providence, 1855.

City Document Number 2, Annual Report of the School Committee of Providence. Providence: Knowles, Anthony & Co., 1854.

Providence Town Tax Records, 1829-1840. Printed by Hutchins and Weeden.

Providence Probate Records (manuscript).

Records of the Boston Selectmen, 1754-1763. Boston, 1887.

Report of the Boston School Committee. Boston, 1855.

Rogers, Horatio, ed. *The Early Records of the Town of Providence*. 20 vols Providence, 1892-1909.

Snow, Edward M., ed. *Census of Rhode Island, 1865*. Providence: Providence Press, 1867.

Secondary Sources-

Articles

Adams, James Truslow. "Disenfranchisement of Negroes in New England." *American Historical Review* 30 (April 1925): 543-47.

Bartlett, Irving H. "The Free Negro in Providence, Rhode Island." *Negro History Bulletin* 14 (December 1950): 51-54, 66, 67.

Cottrol, Robert J. "Heroism and the Origins of Afro-American History." *New England Quarterly* (June 1978): 256-63.

Eitzen, D. Stanley. "Status Inconsistency and Wallace Supporters in a Midwestern City." *Social Forces* 48 (June 1970): 493-98.

Fox, Dixon Ryan. "The Negro Vote in Old New York." In *Free Blacks in America 1800-1860*, pp. 95-112. Edited by John H. Bracey, Eliot

Rudwick, and August Meier. Belmont, Calif.: Wadsworth Publishers, 1970.

Goldin, Claudia Dale. "Family Strategies and the Family Economy in the Late Nineteenth Century: The Role of Secondary Workers." In *Philadelphia: Work Space, Family and Group Experience in the 19th Century*, pp. 277-310. Edited by Theodore Hershberg. New York: Oxford University Press, 1981.

Greene, Lorenzo Johnston. "The New England Negro as Seen in Advertisements for Runaway Slaves." *Journal of Negro History* 29 (December 1969): 125-46.

——. "Slaveholding in New England and Its Awakening." *Journal of Negro History* 13 (October 1928): 492-533.

——. "Some Observations on the Black Regiment of Rhode Island." *Journal of Negro History* 37 (April 1952): 142-72.

Grossman, Lawrence. "George T. Downing and Desegregation of Rhode Island Public Schools, 1855-1866." *Rhode Island History* 36, no. 4 (November 1977): 99-105.

Hershberg, Theodore. "Free Blacks in Antebellum Philadelphia, A Study of Ex-Slaves, Freeborn and Socioeconomic Decline." In *Philadelphia: Work, Space, Family and Group Experience in the 19th Century*, pp. 368-91. Edited by Theodore Hershberg. New York: Oxford University Press, 1981.

Hershberg, Theodore, and Williams, Henry. "Mulattoes and Blacks: Intragroup Color Differences and Social Stratification in Nineteenth Century Philadelphia." In *Philadelphia: Work, Space, Family and Group Experience in the 19th Century*, pp. 392-434. Edited by Theodore Hershberg. New York: Oxford University Press, 1981.

Hershberg, Theodore; Furstenberg, Frank F.; and Model, John. "The Origins of the Female-Headed Black Family: The Impact of the Urban Experience." In *Philadelphia: Work, Space, Family and Group Experience in the 19th Century*, pp. 435-54. Edited by Theodore Hershberg. New York: Oxford University Press, 1981.

Hershberg, Theodore, et al. "A Tale of Three Cities: Blacks, Immigrants and Opportunity in Philadelphia, 1850-1880, 1930, 1970." In *Philadelphia: Work, Space, Family and Group Experience in the 19th Century*, pp. 461-91. Edited by Theodore Hershberg. New York: Oxford University Press, 1981.

Hirsch, Leo H. "New York and the Negro from 1783-1865." *Journal of Negro History* 16 (October 1931): 382-473.

Howland, John. "Thomas Howland and His Portrait." Address before Rhode Island Historical Society, n.d. [nineteenth century].

Lemmons, J. Stanley, and McKenna, A. "Reenfranchisement of Rhode

Island Negroes." *Rhode Island History* 30 (February 1971): 3-13.

Lopreato, Joseph. "Upward Social Mobility and Political Orientation." *American Sociological Review* 32 (August 1967): 586-92.

Platt, Orville H. "Negro Governors." *New Haven Colony Historical Society Papers* 6 (1900): 315-35.

Segal, David R., and Knoke, David. "Social Mobility, Status Inconsistency and Partisan Realignment in the United States." *Social Forces* 47 (December 1968): 154-57.

Silberstein, Fred B., and Seeman, Melvin. "Social Mobility and Prejudice." *American Journal of Sociology* 65 (November 1959): 258-64.

Wesley, Charles H. "Negro Suffrage in the Period of Constitution Making, 1787-1865." *Journal of Negro History* 32 (April 1947): 143-68.

———. "The Negroes of New England in the Emancipation Movement." *Journal of Negro History* 24 (January 1939): 155-99.

———. "The Negroes' Struggle for Freedom in Its Birthplace." *Journal of Negro History* 30 (January 1945): 62-81.

———. "The Participation of Negroes in Anti-Slavery Political Parties." *Journal of Negro History* 29 (January 1944): 32-74.

Wright, Marion Thompson. "Negro Suffrage in New Jersey, 1776-1875." *Journal of Negro History* 33 (April 1948): 168-224.

Books and Dissertations

Adorno, T. W.; Frankel-Brunswick, Else; Levinson, Daniel J.; and Sanford, R. N. *The Authoritarian Personality*. New York: W. W. Norton, 1969.

Arnold, Samuel Greene. *History of the State of Rhode Island and Providence Plantations*. Providence: D. Appleton & Co., 1894.

Bartlett, Irving H. *From Slave to Citizen: The Story of the Negro in Rhode Island*. Providence: Rhode Island Urban League, 1947.

Battle, Charles A. *Negroes on the Island of Rhode Island*. Newport, 1932.

Benson, Lee. *The Concept of Jacksonian Democracy: New York as a Test Cast*. Princeton: Princeton University Press, 1961.

Berlin, Ira. *Slaves without Masters*. New York: Vintage Press, 1974.

Blalock, Hubert M. *Social Statistics*. New York: McGraw-Hill, 1960.

Blassingame, John W. *Black New Orleans, 1860-1880*. Chicago: University of Chicago Press, 1973.

Blum, John M. et al. *The National Experience*. New York: Harcourt Brace & World, 1968.

Brennan, Joseph. *Social Conditions in Industrial Rhode Island, 1820-1860*. Washington, D.C.: Catholic University Press, 1940.

Carpenter, Esther Bernon. *South Country Studies.* Boston: Roberts
    Brothers, 1924.
Chickering, Jesse. *A Statistical View of the Population of Massachusetts,
    1765-1840.* Boston: C. C. Little & J. Brown, 1846.
Coleman, Peter J. *The Transformation of Rhode Island.* Providence:
    Brown University Press, 1963.
Coser, Lewis A. *The Functions of Social Conflict.* Glencoe, Ill.: Free Press,
    1956.
Cottrol, Robert J. "Black Providence, 1800-1860: A Community's For-
    mation" Ph.D. dissertation, Yale University, 1978.
Cox, Peter R. *Demography.* New York: Cambridge University Press,
    1970.
Cruse, Harold. *The Crisis of the Negro Intellectual.* New York: William
    Morrow & Co., 1967.
Daniels, John. *In Freedom's Birthplace: A Study of the Boston Negroes.*
    New York: Arno Press, 1969.
Davis, David Brian. *The Problem of Slavery in the Age of Revolution,
    1770-1823.* Ithaca: Cornell University Press, 1975.
David, Lance E. et al. *American Economic Growth: An Economist's
    History of the United States.* New York: Harper and Row, 1972.
Degler, Carl N. *Neither Black nor White: Slavery and Race Relations in
    Brazil and the United States.* New York: Macmillan, 1971.
Dennison, George M. *The Dorr War.* Lexington: University of Kentucky
    Press, 1976.
Dollard. John. *Caste and Class in a Southern Town.* New York: Double-
    day, 1957.
Dorr, Henry. *The Planting and Growth of Providence.* Providence: S. S.
    Rider, 1882.
Drake, St. Clair, and Cayton, Horace R. *Black Metropolis.* Vol. 1. New
    York: Harcourt, Brace & Co., 1945.
Du Bois, W. E. B. *The Philadelphia Negro.* New York: Schocken Books,
    1967.
Elkins, Stanley. *Slavery: A Problem in American Institutional and In-
    tellectual Life.* New York: Grosset & Dunlap, 1963.
Fish, Carl Russel. *The Rise of the Common Man.* New York: Macmillan,
    1927.
Floud, Roderick. *An Introduction to Quantitative Methods for Historians.*
    Princeton: Princeton University Press, 1973.
Frazier, E. Franklin. *The Negro Church in America.* New York: Schocken
    Books, 1974.
Gambino, Richard. *Blood of My Blood: The Dilemma of the Italian Ameri-
    cans.* Garden City, N.Y.: Doubleday, 1975.

Gettleman, Marvin E. *The Dorr Rebellion*. New York: Random House, 1973.

Greene, Evarts B., and Harrington, Virginia. *American Population before the Federal Census of 1790*. New York: Columbia University Press, 1932.

Greene, Lorenzo Johnston. *The Negro in Colonial New England, 1620-1776*. New York: Columbia University Press, 1968.

Handlin, Oscar. *Boston's Immigrants, 1790-1865: A Study in Acculturation*. Cambridge: Harvard University Press, 1959.

Hazard, Caroline. *College Tom: A Study of Life in Narragansett in XVIII Century*. Boston: Houghton Mifflin & Co., 1893.

Henning, Basil Duke et al. *Crises in English History, 1066-1945*. New York: Holt, Rinehart & Co. 1964.

Horton, James Oliver, and Horton, Lois E. *Black Bostonians: Family Life and Community Struggle in the Antebellum North*. New York: Holmes and Meir, 1979.

Johnson, James Weldon. *Black Manhattan*. New York: Arno Press, 1968.

Johnston, William Dawson. *Slavery in Rhode Island, 1775-1776*. Providence: Rhode Island Historical Society, 1894.

Jones, Augustine. *Moses Brown*. Providence: Rhode Island Printing Co., 1892.

Jordan, Winthrop. *White over Black: American Attitudes toward the Negro, 1550-1812*. Chapel Hill: University of North Carolina Press, 1968.

Kimball, Gertrude Selwyn. *Providence in Colonial Times*. Boston: Houghton Mifflin & Co., 1912.

Kiven, Arline Ruth. *Then Why the Negroes*. Providence: Urban League of Rhode Island, 1973.

Lipset, Seymour Martin, and Bendix, Reinhard. *Social Mobility in Industrial Society*. Berkeley: University of California Press, 1967.

Litwack, Leon F. *North of Slavery*. Chicago: University of Chicago Press, 1961.

Lopreato, Joseph, and Hazelrigg, Lawrence E. *Class, Conflict and Mobility*. San Francisco: Chandler, 1972.

McManus, Edgar J. *A History of Negro Slavery in New York:* Syracuse: Syracuse University Press, 1966.

——. *Black Bondage in the North*. Syracuse: Syracuse University Press, 1973.

Maxey, Edwin. *Suffrage Extension in Rhode Island down to 1848*. Lincoln, Neb., 1908.

Merton, Robert K. *Social Theory and Social Structure*. New York: Free Press, 1968.

Moore, George H. *Historical Notes on the Employment of Negroes in the American Army of the Revolution.* New York: Charles T. Evans, 1862.

——. *Notes on the History of Slavery in Massachusetts.* New York: D. Appleton & Co., 1866.

Morgan, Edmund S. *American Slavery, American Freedom: The Ordeal of Colonial Virginia.* New York: W. W. Norton, 1975.

——. *The Puritan Family.* Boston: Trustees of the Public Library, 1944.

Mowry, Arthur. *The Dorr War.* Providence: Preston & Rounds Co., 1901.

Nell, William C. *The Colored Patriots of the American Revolution.* Boston: R. F. Wallcut, 1855.

Nie, Norman H. et al. *Statistical Package for the Social Sciences.* New York: McGraw-Hill, 1975.

Notestein, Wallace. *The English People on the Eve of Colonization.* New York: Harper, 1954.

Ottley, Roi, and Weatherby, William J., eds. *The Negro in New York.* New York: Praeger, 1967.

Palfrey, John Gorham. *History of New England.* Vol. 5. Boston: Little, Brown, 1890.

Pease, Jane Hanna. "The Freshness of Fanaticism. Abby Kelly Foster: An Essay in Reform." Ph.D. dissertation, University of North Carolina, 1969.

Peterson, Edward. *History of Rhode Island.* New York: J. S. Taylor, 1853.

Pleck, Elizabeth Hafkin. *Black Migration and Poverty: Boston, 1865-1900.* New York: Academic Press, 1979.

Quadro, David Francis. "An Analysis of the Arguments Used in the Senate Debates on Negro Suffrage." Ph.D. dissertation, University of California at Los Angeles, 1972.

Quarles, Benjamin. *The Negro in the American Revolution.* Chapel Hill: University of North Carolina Press, 1961.

Rabinowitz, Howard N. *Race Relations in the Urban South, 1865-1890.* New York: Oxford University Press, 1978.

Ravitch, Diane. *The Great School Wars.* New York: Basic Books, 1974.

Richards, Leonard L. *Gentlemen of Property and Standing: Anti-Abolition Mobs in America.* New York: Oxford University Press, 1970.

Rider, Sidney S. *An Historical Inquiry Concerning the Attempt to Raise a Regiment of Slaves by Rhode Island.* Providence: Rhode Island Historical Society Publications, 1880.

Robinson, William H. *Blacks in 19th Century Rhode Island: An Overview.* Providence: Rhode Island Black Heritage Society, 1978.

Salvador, George Arnold. *Paul Cuffe: The Black Yankee.* New Bedford, Mass.: Reynolds-Dewalt Printing, 1969.

Schlesinger, Arthur M., Jr. *The Age of Jackson.* Boston: Little, Brown, 1945.

Shorter, Edwin. *The Historian and the Computer.* Englewood Cliffs, N.J.: Prentice-Hall, 1971.

Smith, Abbot Emerson. *Colonists in Bondage: White Servitude and Convict Labor in America, 1607-1776.* Chapel Hill: University of North Carolina Press, 1942.

Spear, Allan H. *Black Chicago: The Making of a Negro Ghetto, 1890-1920.* Chicago: University of Chicago Press, 1967.

Stanley, John Langley. "Majority Tyranny in Tocqueville's America: The Failure of Negro Suffrage in New York State in 1846." Ph.D. dissertation, Cornell University, 1966.

Steiner, Bernard C. *History of Slavery in Connecticut.* Baltimore: Johns Hopkins, 1893.

Stockwell, Thomas B. *A History of Public Education in Rhode Island.* Providence: Providence Press Co., 1876.

Thernstrom, Stephan. *Poverty and Progress: Social Mobility in a Nineteenth Century City.* Cambridge: Harvard University Press, 1964.

——. *The Other Bostonians: Poverty and Progress in the American Metropolis, 1880-1970.* Cambridge: Harvard University Press, 1973.

Thompson, Mack. *Moses Brown: Reluctant Reformer.* Chapel Hill: University of North Carolina Press, 1962.

Tyler, Alice Felt. *Freedom's Ferment.* New York: Harper, 1962.

Van den Berghe, Pierre. *Race and Racism.* New York: Wiley, 1967.

Wade, Richard C. *Slavery in the Cities.* New York: Oxford University Press, 1964.

Warner, Robert Austin. *New Haven Negroes: A Social History.* New Haven: Yale University Press, 1940.

Weeden, William B. *Early Rhode Island.* New York: Grafton Press, 1910.

Wells, Ida A. "A Survey of the Negro Problem in the United States as Seen by British Travellers to America, 1800-1861." Ph.D. dissertation, Northern Illinois University, 1969.

White, Arthur Owen. "Blacks and Education in Antebellum Massachusetts: Strategies for Social Mobility." Ed. D. dissertation, State University of New York at Buffalo, 1971.

Wilbur, Benjamin Franklin. *Little Compton Families: Little Compton, Rhode Island.* Little Compton: Little Compton Historical Society, 1974.

Williams, George W. *History of the Negro Race in America from 1619-1880.* Vols. 1-2. New York: G. P. Putnam's Sons, 1883.

Woodward, C. Vann. *The Strange Career of Jim Crow.* New York: Oxford University Press, 1957.

Woodward, Carl N. *Plantation in Yankeeland: The Story of Cocumscussoc, Mirror of Colonial Rhode Island.* Chester, Conn.: Pequot Press, 1971.

Wrigley, E. A. *Population and History.* London: Weidenfield & Nicolson, 1969.

INDEX

About the Author

ROBERT J. COTTROL is Assistant Dean for Arts and Sciences and Lecturer in History at Georgetown University. His articles and essays on Afro-American and American History have appeared in *The Journal of Black Studies*, *New England Quarterly*, and *Tulane Law Review*.